Issues Now in the News

Adam Worcester

W9-CEL-885

Second Edition

Compass Publishing

Issues Now in the News Second Edition

Adam Worcester

© 2008 Compass Publishing

All rights reserved. No part of this book may be
reproduced, stored in a retrieval system, or transmitted
in any form or by any means, electronic, mechanical,
photocopying, recording, or otherwise, without prior
permission in writing from the publisher.

Acquisitions Editors: David Charlton, Jenna Myers
Development Editor: Vinodini Murugesan
Cover/Interior Design: Dammora Inc.

email: info@compasspub.com
http://www.compasspub.com

ISBN: 978-1-59966-361-6

10 9 8 7 6 5 4 3 2 1
10 09 08

Photo Credits
• Cover © Yonhap News
• p.   111 © Shutterstock, Inc.
• pp. 14, 15, 68, 69, 110, 141 © European Pressphoto Agency
• p.   129 © The New York Times
• p.   116 © www.amazonteam.org
• pp. 75, 87, 93 © Inmagine Corp LLC
• pp. 121, 123 © JupiterImages Corporation
• pp. 7, 8, 9, 13, 19, 21, 25, 26, 27, 31, 32, 33,
        37, 38, 39, 43, 44, 45, 49, 50, 51, 57, 62, 63, 73, 74,
        80, 81, 85, 91, 92, 97, 98, 99, 103, 104, 105, 115,
        117, 122, 128, 133, 134, 135, 140, 145, 146, 147,
        151, 152, 153, 157 © Yonhap News

Every effort has been made to trace all sources of illustrations/photos/information
in this book, but if any have been inadvertently overlooked, the publisher will be
pleased to make the necessary arrangements at the first opportunity.

Table of Contents

16198177585

Introduction

Issues Now in the News is a 25-unit course-book designed to bring current events of worldwide interest and concern into the English-language classroom. Each unit focuses on an article originally produced for Voice of America (VOA). Voice of America (www.voanews.com), which first went on the air in 1942, is a multimedia international broadcasting service funded by the US government through the Broadcasting Board of Governors. VOA broadcasts more than 1,000 hours of news, information, educational, and cultural programming every week to an estimated worldwide audience of more than 115 million people.

Selected news articles are drawn from diverse nations and cultures and have been carefully chosen to provide a wide range of interesting topics. Each unit is methodically planned around the central topic to engage students' interest while improving general knowledge and providing useful language practice. Each article is accompanied by full-color photographs drawn primarily from news photo or agency services; these images have been carefully selected to highlight and clarify the content of each article. The goal of this text is to inspire and encourage students to take an interest in issues that are of global importance — i.e. politics, lifestyle choices, culture, ecology, economy, climatology, the environment, etc. — and to discuss aspects of these issues in an English-language context.

Issues Now in the News is an excellent resource for English-language instruction for students at more advanced levels, especially in college or university settings. Because the source material for this book was created for a native English-speaking audience, the language used is elevated and topic-specific, which facilitates the learning of vocabulary in a real world context for foreigner second-language learners. The beginning of each unit introduces the topic, highlights key points to notice, and provides background information on the topic in order to contextualize the subject matter. The reading text is followed by activities which are specifically designed to promote vocabulary learning and retention through reading, writing, and discussion. Another attractive feature of ***Issues Now in the News*** is that audio recordings of the articles are provided along with text transcripts. This combination of listening, reading, and writing activities mutually reinforces overall learning and retention of the integrated materials. Taken as a whole, with the topics for guided discussion at the end of each unit serving as a stimulus for spoken language, this course-book leaves nothing to be desired in terms of language focus and cognitive content for more advanced English-language learners.

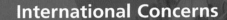

Immigration Debate

Warm-up

The U.S. and European governments wish to place restrictions on immigration into their countries from poorer neighboring regions. Many of the citizens in richer nations resent the entry of unskilled laborers into their countries. These citizens feel the newcomers rely on taxpayer money and charity to survive. Skilled and educated workers are generally more welcome. Immigrants are protesting the attempts by governments to stop them from gaining entry to, and building a life in, countries with more successful economies. They contend such policies are unfair and cruel and that they have the right to try to earn a living.

Is there a place for immigrants in developed nations? Experts disagree.

Points to Notice

As you read, pay attention to the information and opinions associated with each of the following people:

- Amirouche Laradjane — Algerian illegal immigrant in France
- Nicolas Sarkozy — French Interior Minister
- Francis Barjot — Catholic priest at Saint Hippolyte Church in Paris
- Daniele Joly — Head of the Centre for Research and Ethnic Relations
- Bakari Coulibali — a Muslim immigrant from Bamako, Mali
- Hans Entzinger — Immigration expert at Erasmus University

Cultural Notes and Background

Some immigrants consider themselves refugees fleeing corrupt governments. Many immigrants are simply moving from poorer neighboring nations in search of better opportunities and a higher standard of living. In the past, people could move around the world freely, and entry or exit between countries was not regulated. These days, however, there are strict regulations in place. That is why travelers all carry passports that are stamped by immigration officials when they travel, and why they are issued visas that allow them to stay in a country legally for only a limited period of time. A working visa, or American "green card," is a permit allowing one to work legally in a country of which one is not a citizen. Without such a visa, a person breaks the law by taking up employment.

Immigration Debate Stirring on Both Sides of Atlantic

The immigration debate is heating up on both sides of the Atlantic, pitting advocates for legalizing illegal immigrants against those who support stronger anti-immigration measures. In the United States, more than a million people 5 *marched last week to demand greater immigrant rights. The welcome mat is vanishing for immigrants in large parts of Western Europe, at least for low-skilled foreign workers living in the region illegally.* 10

At breakfast for the homeless at Saint Hippolyte Roman Catholic church in Paris, Algerian immigrant Amirouche Laradjane munches on a thick 15 slice of bread as he discusses new French legislation aimed at tightening immigration rules.

Laradjane, who has been living illegally in France for the 20 past three years, calls the draft bill shameful. He says France's center-right government is fascist. And he says the bill's author, Interior Minister Nicolas 25 Sarkozy, who is of Hungarian extraction, had forgotten his own immigrant roots.

The immigration legislation is now being examined by 30 France's parliament. If passed, it would make it harder for illegal foreigners like Laradjane to gain residency, and for families of immigrants to settle here. The bill also aims to select out 35 highly skilled workers from blue-collared ones like Laradjane, who works in construction.

Sarkozy says the bill will reduce rising anti-immigration sentiments in France, while also

Thousands of demonstrators march through the streets of downtown Los Angeles May 1, 2006, as part of what is being billed as 'A Day Without Immigrants,' a nationwide protest staged by immigrant rights advocates to protest proposed legislation to reform U.S. immigration law.

(REUTERS/Lucas Jackson)

responding to skilled labor shortages in certain 40 economic sectors. He describes the legislation as balanced and just.

But critics call the bill mean-spirited and unfair. Christian churches have taken a leading role in demanding the legislation be softened. Clerics 45 like Francis Barjot, parish priest at Saint Hippolyte, worry about the future of illegal immigrants in France.

Father Barjot believes the legislation will pass. He fears that in a few years 50 France will enact even tougher legislation against illegal immigrants, forcing them to sink even further in the shadows. 55

Many French churches have offered shelter to these illegal immigrants, including Saint Hippolyte, located in a heavily Chinese neighborhood 60 in southern Paris. Last week, 150 foreigners came there to seek a place to stay, and to air their protests against the immigration legislation. 65 Father Barjot took them in, offering a bed to some and free breakfast to everyone.

As he sipped a large bowl of coffee and milk, 70 Bakari Coulibali, 45, said he was grateful for the church's generosity.

"I thank these Christians," says Coulibali, who is a Muslim from Bamako, Mali. "In the morning, we 75 all get coffee and a piece of bread. What do we have besides this?" he asks. "Nothing."

A one-time farmer outside Bamako, Coulibali emigrated to France 16 years ago, hoping to find a

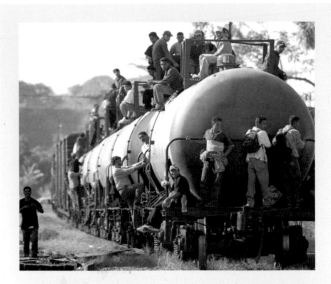

Dozens of Central American citizens hang off a train in Tapachula, Chiapas, Mexico, en route to the U.S., in this January, 2003, file photo. Immigration rights activists report that more than 400 migrants are known to have died in the last year, as people are forced to take more dangerous mountain and desert routes since U.S. security tightened its measures against undocumented immigration.

(AP Photo/Juan de Dios Garcia)

better job and life. He has found work here and there — in construction, cleaning houses, emptying trash. But today, Coulibali is homeless and without legal working papers; his future is bleak.

"I want legal papers to work like everyone else," he said. "We want our papers."

France is not alone in trying to select out its immigrants. Increasingly, experts say, European governments are introducing new immigration tests and other screening devices to attract only the brightest and most qualified workers. In principle at least, the attitudes toward unqualified and illegal foreigners is hardening, says Daniele Joly, head of the Centre for Research in Ethnic Relations at the University of Warwick in England.

"There is a general trend of regulating and restricting immigration, and in particular asylum [seekers]," she said. "But also illegal immigration. The door, in appearance, is closed to immigration and the discourse of politicians is very hostile to immigration."

The Netherlands and Germany have passed new screening tests to draw in skilled workers and those who share their social and political values. The European Union is also considering a similar integration contract.

Spain and Greece have granted amnesty to several million illegal immigrants, but they continue to ship many others home. Even countries like Denmark, with a history of openness toward immigrants, are closing up their borders.

Unlike the United States, fear of tighter immigration restrictions has not sparked massive rallies in Europe. Hans Entzinger, an immigration expert at Erasmus University Rotterdam, in the Netherlands, explains why.

"Illegal immigrants are very poorly organized, almost by definition. And no one takes an interest in them," he said. "This has to do with general anti-immigration feelings. It's very difficult to find an organization that defends the rights of illegal immigrants."

In France, high unemployment and last autumn's riots by ethnic immigrant youths have sharpened anti-immigration sentiments. Many recent surveys show strong support for tighter immigration measures, the bread and butter rhetoric of the far right.

Indeed, a poll published Friday in *Le Figaro* magazine found Jean-Marie Le Pen, head of the far-right National Front party, coasting on an 18 percent approval rating — slightly higher than in 2002, when he placed second in French presidential elections. Le Pen, 77, is now stumping for next year's presidential race with a new slogan: "France, Love It or Leave It."

Sarkozy, another presidential hopeful, is also borrowing some of Le Pen's rhetoric, experts say.

Anti-immigration sentiments are similarly feeding far-right parties in Germany, the Netherlands, Denmark, Austria, and Britain — where the British National Party doubled its number of local councilors in English elections Thursday.

Still, immigration experts like Daniele Joly say the tough talk in Europe is not always matched by action. Britain, for example, delivered 400,000 work permits to immigrants last year alone. At the end of the day, she says, European politicians and economists realize, with the continent's population declining, they need more immigration, including unskilled workers.

By Lisa Bryant Paris 06 May 2006
Voice of America

nter-right government
the bill's
the immigration legisl
Father Barjot took them
offering a bed to some

Words and Idioms

Vocabulary
Match each word to its definition.

1. immigration *(n)* ●
2. illegally *(adv)* ●
3. blue-collar *(adj)* ●
4. sentiment *(n)* ●
5. homeless *(adj)* ●
6. unqualified *(adj)* ●

● a. to limit; to prevent
● b. a march or meeting organized to protest something
● c. the political language of an argument
● d. a legal agreement between two or more parties
● e. an expert who studies money matters, business, and finance
● f. a person who asks permission to live in another country, usually due to political dangers in the home country

7. restrict *(v)* ●

● g. a pardon granted by a government to lawbreakers, usually for political offenses

8. asylum seeker *(n)* ●
9. hostile *(adj)* ●
10. skilled *(adj)* ●
11. contract *(n)* ●
12. amnesty *(n)* ●
13. border *(n)* ●
14. rally *(n)* ●
15. rhetoric *(n)* ●
16. economist *(n)* ●
17. permit *(n)* ●

● h. the frontier line separating one country from another
● i. being trained, able, qualified, or talented
● j. without education and training in a specific field
● k. being without a house or apartment to live in
● l. negative; unfriendly; aggressive
● m. the movement of people into one nation from another
● n. a document that grants official permission to do something
● o. an emotion; a feeling or set of feelings
● p. in a manner that breaks the law
● q. related to workers whose jobs involve manual labor

Idioms and Expressions
Fill in the blanks with the correct idiom or expression.

the welcome mat is vanishing: to be no longer welcome where one once was
The welcome mat has vanished at Tom's new job because he hasn't produced the necessary sales.

to take (someone) in: to offer someone food and shelter; to care for someone
I took in my sister's orphaned children after her death.

bread and butter: the basic and most important source of income
The bread and butter of a mechanic's job is fixing leaky exhaust pipes.

1. As a freelance writer, writing catalogues is how I earn my _____.

2. After my divorce from Frank, _____ at his parents' home.

3. Are you planning to _____ the stray puppy I found on your doorstep?

Exploring Content

A. Two of the following statements are FALSE according to the passage. Check (✔) the FALSE statements.

1. __ More than one million Americans marched to protest new legislation granting immigrants special rights.

2. __ France's interior minister, Nicolas Sarkozy, wants to be France's next president.

3. __ Christian churches in France don't want to help illegal immigrants.

4. __ Last year, the British government issued 400,000 work permits to immigrants.

Rewrite the FALSE statements using information from the passage to make them TRUE.

a) _____

b) _____

B. Choose the best answer.

1. What is the main idea of the article?
   a. Immigrants are welcome in developed countries if they are skilled.
   b. Working illegally is inevitable for foreign immigrants in Europe and the U.S.
   c. Immigration is a worldwide problem, and most countries hate immigrants.
   d. Immigration is a complex problem that cannot be easily resolved.

2. What can be inferred about Jean-Marie Le Pen?
   a. He is strongly in favor of immigration.
   b. He wants Nicolas Sarkozy to become France's next president.
   c. He needs 18 percent approval to introduce new anti-immigration legislation.
   d. He wants to be France's next president.

3. Read the following sentence:

   "Anti-immigration sentiments are similarly feeding far-right parties in Germany, the Netherlands, Denmark, Austria, and Britain — where the British National Party doubled its number of local councilors in English elections Thursday."

   Which of the following sentences best expresses the essential information in the above sentence?
   a. Local councilors from far-right parties are feeding poor immigrants in Germany, the Netherlands, Denmark, Austria, and Britain.
   b. The British National Party held an election in which immigrants became local councilors.
   c. Conservative political parties in Europe are becoming more powerful because more people are supporting their anti-immigration sentiments.
   d. Anti-immigration sentiments help far-right parties to double their councilors in elections.

Summary & Discussion

Summary
Fill in the blanks.

welcome mat	take them in	illegally	borders	blue-collar
skilled	immigration	sentiments	restrict	hostile

Immigrants who are living in European countries **1** _____ are finding that the **2** _____ has been removed. Far-right political parties are trying to pass legislation that keeps them from crossing **3** _____ and entering these nations. Most immigrants are unskilled, **4** _____ workers who are looking for job opportunities. However, negative **5** _____ from the citizens and conservative politicians are making life hard for these immigrants. Often, their only hope is charity from institutions, like the Catholic Church, which **6** _____ and offer them basic food and shelter. Illegal immigrants have a hard time understanding the **7** _____ attitude towards them. All they want is to have an opportunity for a better life. Instead, far-right parties that support anti-immigration laws want to **8** _____ the entry of foreigners. Immigrants are generally only welcome if they are **9** _____ professionals; unskilled workers have a much harder time surviving. The trend towards an anti-**10** _____ stance tends to be overtaking Europe, and also the U.S. to some degree.

Discussion
Discuss these questions with your class.

1. Would you consider immigrating to another country? Why or why not?

2. Do you think illegal immigrants in the U.S. and Europe have a right to be there? Justify your answer.

3. Do you think illegal immigrants have become a social problem in your country?

4. Explain the difference between an illegal immigrant and a refugee.

Automakers Going Green

Warm-up

As gasoline prices soar toward $4 a gallon in the United States, automobile manufacturers are working harder than ever to develop and sell fuel-efficient vehicles. These fall into three primary categories: 1) cars and trucks that get more miles per gallon of gas; 2) new types of vehicles that use fuels other than gasoline; and 3) electric and hybrid cars, which rely completely or partially on electricity.

Points to Notice

As you read, consider the comments made by Troy Clarke, General Motors North America president, and Paul Eisenstein, a longtime automotive writer. What does Clarke say about the future of US automobiles? What does Eisenstein claim about the US demand for large vehicles? What does Eisenstein pose as the current dilemma for US automakers?

Cultural Notes and Background

America depends on the automobile more than any other country. In 2006, there were about 137 million autos in the United States. More than sixty-five percent of American households own more than one vehicle, and in many families there is one car for each person old enough to drive. The average American drives his or her car about 13,000 miles a year, and consumes nearly 550 annual gallons of gas. Between 1992 and 2005, the number of alternative-fuel cars in the US, including electric cars, more than doubled. In 1992, there were only about 1,600 electric cars in America. By 2006, there were nearly 51,500.

Automakers Show Off Green, Fuel-Efficient Vehicles

More than 6,700 reporters from forty-two nations are in Detroit for the news media preview of that city's North American International Auto Show, which opens to the general public this weekend. This year's show emphasizes fuel efficiency and green technology, but, as VOA's Greg Flakus reports from Detroit, there are also plenty of big glitzy cars and trucks on display.

On display in Detroit's downtown Cobo Convention Center are 700 vehicles from all the major automakers, including local companies like General Motors, Ford and Chrysler, and companies from China, Japan, and Europe. Around fifty new vehicles are being introduced by various manufacturers.

US automakers are making a big effort this year to go green, showing off many varieties of low-emission, fuel-efficient vehicles, including hybrids, fuel-cell cars, and vehicles that run on ethanol and bio-diesel fuels. General Motors announced that it has invested heavily in Cosaka Incorporated, an Illinois firm that claims to have developed a cost-cutting technology for producing ethanol, an alcohol fuel produced from plant material.

Most ethanol today is produced from corn, but Cosaka plans on using waste material like corn stalks and wood chips.

General Motors North America President, Troy Clarke, tells VOA that his company sees a need to move away from reliance on gasoline as the only fuel for its cars.

"The next 25 years, maybe even longer, looks a lot like the early part of the (20th) century in the auto industry," Clarke said.

Peter Horbury, Executive Director of design, Ford Motor Company, introduced the 2008 Lincoln MKT concept car during the North American International Auto Show in Detroit, Michigan on January 14, 2008.

(EPA/Charlie Cortez)

"There will be a lot of different propulsion systems. Ninety-six percent of the vehicles in the US today are moved by gasoline. We need to diversify that."

Clarke says his industry has been wrongly criticized for being slow to innovate. He says General Motors began developing an electric car many years ago and has also developed other kinds of fuel-efficient vehicles.

"Now we have eight hybrids in the market today," he said. "We have 16 on the way between now and, I think, the end of next year, and we can compete very effectively in the hybrid area. But we really have never given up on our vision of an electric vehicle."

General Motors is still testing a new battery to power the Chevrolet Volt, an advanced electric hybrid that was first shown here last year, but which may not be ready for market for a few more years.

Veteran automotive journalist Paul Eisenstein, who writes for *The Car Connection.com*, says car makers use the North American International Auto Show to introduce such innovations and get the word out to people around the world.

"This is a place that the manufacturers come, not just to talk to consumers directly, but to talk to a global media," Eisenstein said. "This is a place where they can get to everyone from the small bloggers in the Czech Republic to the big networks here in North America. It is no wonder that virtually every manufacturer in the world is here, including five of the Chinese manufacturers that are looking to try to get into the North American market over the next couple of years."

While automakers are emphasizing fuel efficiency and reduced carbon emissions this year, they are also showing off a lot of big cargo pick up trucks, sport utility vehicles and gas-

The Jeep Renegade concept is introduced during the North American International Auto Show in Detroit, Michigan on January 14, 2008.

(EPA/Rob Widdis)

guzzling luxury cars. Paul Eisenstein says that is simply a response to continuing demand for those vehicles.

"The reality is Americans like big, they like power, they like performance, they like towing and cargo-hauling and people-hauling capabilities," he said. "So for anybody to say we should stop producing these big trucks and go to produce these small, high-mileage cars, is ridiculous. The market is there for the big vehicles."

Eisenstein says US car makers are trying to satisfy the demand for larger vehicles, while at the same time trying to meet new regulations from Washington that require them to improve fuel efficiency. That could be a real challenge for an industry that is already struggling to keep up with foreign competition.

The North American International Auto Show began in Detroit as a local event in 1907. The event went international twenty years ago, but it is still organized locally by the Detroit Auto Dealers Association.

By Greg Flakus Detroit 14 January 2008
Voice of America

Vocabulary
Match each word to its definition.

1. green *(adj)* ●	● a. a combination of two different technologies
2. glitzy *(adj)* ●	● b. to display proudly
3. emission *(n)* ●	● c. aim or goal
4. hybrid *(n)* ●	● d. extravagant
5. stalk *(n)* ●	● e. to consume a lot quickly
6. propulsion *(n)* ●	● f. healthy for the natural environment
7. diversify *(v)* ●	● g. laughable; not serious
8. innovate *(v)* ●	● h. to increase variety
9. vision *(n)* ●	● i. main stem of a plant
10. blogger *(n)* ●	● j. person who writes regularly on the Internet
11. show off *(v phrase)* ●	● k. pollution from auto engines
12. cargo *(n)* ●	● l. to pull another vehicle along behind
13. guzzle *(v)* ●	● m. the action of propelling
14. tow *(v)* ●	● n. the goods or merchandise transported in a vehicle
15. ridiculous *(adj)* ●	● o. to do something in a new way

Idioms and Expressions
Fill in the blanks with the correct idiom or expression.

open to: to become available or accessible
The play opened to critics last night.

go green: to operate in an environmentally friendly manner
The company is going green by producing less waste.

get the word out: to generate publicity
We need to get the word out on the danger of bird flu.

1. We are _____ by buying longer-lasting light bulbs.

2. The restaurant will be _____ the public on June 14th.

3. We need to _____: Ms. Rogers is leaving the company.

Exploring Content

A. Two of the following statements are FALSE according to the passage. Check (✔) the FALSE statements.

1. __ General Motors has invested a lot of money in a firm that says it can make ethanol cheaply.
2. __ According to Paul Eisenstein, Americans' demand for large vehicles is rapidly declining.
3. __ Troy Clarke agrees with critics who say that General Motors has been slow to develop alternate-fuel cars.
4. __ The North American International Auto Show has been held in Detroit for more than 100 years.

Rewrite the FALSE statements using information from the passage to make them TRUE.

a) _____

b) _____

B. Choose the best answer.

1. What is the main idea of the article?
   a. The North American International Auto Show is the best way to inform people throughout the world about vehicle innovations.
   b. General Motors is bringing sixteen new hybrids to the market next year – including Volt, an all-electric car.
   c. The theme of this year's North American International Auto Show is fuel efficiency and green technology.
   d. Although there are many green vehicles at this year's North American International Auto Show, the emphasis is on large sport utility vehicles.

2. What can be inferred about hybrid vehicles?
   a. They are the most popular type of car on the American market.
   b. There is fierce competition to produce these types of cars.
   c. Manufacturers agree that ethanol is the best type of hybrid fuel.
   d. Americans do not care about fuel efficiency and protecting the environment.

3. Read the following sentence:

   "Eisenstein says US car makers are trying to satisfy the demand for larger vehicles, while at the same time trying to meet new regulations from Washington that require them to improve fuel efficiency."

   Which of the following sentences best expresses the essential information in the above sentence?
   a. American auto manufactures are caught in a dilemma between conflicting demands from consumers and government.
   b. New government rules will soon force many US car makers out of business.
   c. Eisenstein says that American consumers will continue to want larger and larger vehicles, so it's pointless for auto manufacturers to comply with government regulations.
   d. New government regulations will increase US consumer demand for fuel-efficient vehicles, according to Eisenstein.

Summary
Fill in the blanks.

showing off	hybrid	ridiculous	diversify	cargo
move away from	going green	emission	guzzlers	opened to

"1 _____" could be the theme for this year's North American International Auto Show, which recently 2 _____ the general public. Though US car makers are 3 _____ a wide variety of low-4 _____, fuel-efficient 5 _____ vehicles, there are also plenty of traditional large gas-6 _____ on display. Troy Clarke, president of General Motors North America, said American car manufacturers need to 7 _____ their dependence on gasoline and 8 _____ the US market. But, automotive journalist Paul Eisenstein noted that American consumers still want large vehicles with the capability to haul plenty of people and 9 _____. He said it would be 10 _____ for car makers to suddenly stop producing such vehicles.

Discussion
Discuss these questions with your class.

1. What do you know about electric cars and other hybrid vehicles?

2. Which types of hybrid vehicles are available in your country?

3. Besides cars, what are some other ways that your country is "going green"?

4. Can you think of some other ways in which people could help the environment?

Foreign Aid

Warm-up

Developed nations have been attempting to alleviate poverty in the world's poorest countries for decades by donating large sums of money to their governments. The money is intended to stimulate the economies of underdeveloped nations and to build up infrastructure such as schools and hospitals. Unfortunately, this money often ends up being used ineffectively or stolen by corrupt officials. Another problem is that poorer countries sometimes become dependent on the donated money. Consequently, a number of economic experts argue that in the long run, providing foreign aid doesn't really help underdeveloped nations. Those who do believe in foreign aid, on the other hand, argue the funds must just be more carefully monitored to ensure they are used effectively.

Points to Notice

As you read, pay attention to the information and opinions associated with each of the following people:

• Michael Radew — a Senior Fellow with the World Policy Institute
• Steve Radelet — a Senior Fellow at the Center for Global Development
• Luca Barbone — Director of the World Bank's Poverty Reduction Program
• George Ayitey — an economist at the American University
• Mohamed Akhter — President of InterAction, a humanitarian organization

Cultural Notes and Background

Foreign aid refers to very large sums of money given to poor countries that have serious economic problems. The money is intended to assist the poor in areas such as health and education and to start up industries that can generate money so that the underdeveloped nations can become self sufficient. Many rich nations feel indirectly responsible for the poverty of poorer countries in Africa, South America, or Asia since these countries were previously colonized by them and exploited for cheap labor or natural resources. For others, it is a moral issue: those with more should help those with less. The problem is that corruption is rife in the governments of these poorer nations. Often, the money doesn't reach those it is intended for. Instead, it is stolen or badly administered.

Does Foreign Aid Work?

For decades, the international community has pumped massive amounts of money into the world's poorest countries to help promote development and fight poverty. But some critics charge that foreign aid has proven ineffective. ⁵

According to the United States Agency for International Development, or U.S.A.I.D., western countries have spent more than one trillion dollars in grants and loans to 70 countries since the early 1950s to help reduce poverty. But ¹⁰ some critics say such foreign aid has failed to pull the world's poorest nations out of poverty and should be stopped altogether.

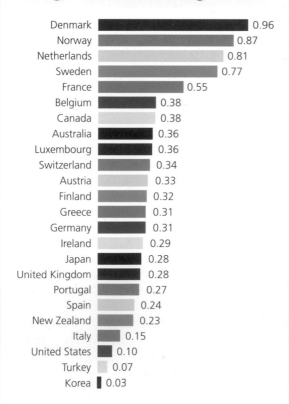

Foreign Aid as Percentage of GDP

Denmark	0.96
Norway	0.87
Netherlands	0.81
Sweden	0.77
France	0.55
Belgium	0.38
Canada	0.38
Australia	0.36
Luxembourg	0.36
Switzerland	0.34
Austria	0.33
Finland	0.32
Greece	0.31
Germany	0.31
Ireland	0.29
Japan	0.28
United Kingdom	0.28
Portugal	0.27
Spain	0.24
New Zealand	0.23
Italy	0.15
United States	0.10
Turkey	0.07
Korea	0.03

The chart above shows the percentage of the Gross Domestic Product (GDP) these countries spend on foreign aid annually.

(Courtesy of VOA)

A Mixed Bag

Michael Radew, a Senior Fellow with The ¹⁵ World Policy Institute in New York says research shows that foreign aid is ineffective and may even be harmful.

"It encourages all the wrong economic policies that made those countries poor in the first place. ²⁰ It strengthens the role of the state sector and of those who control it, who are generally unelected, incompetent, and corrupt officials. It actually disadvantages the large majority of the population, especially the rural population," says Mr. Radew. ²⁵

But other analysts contend that foreign aid has produced mixed results, depending on where and how the funds are spent. They note that Taiwan and South Korea, for example, used foreign aid successfully, eventually becoming ³⁰ donors themselves.

Steve Radelet, a Senior Fellow at the Center for Global Development in Washington, D.C. says aid is least effective in countries such as Somalia and Haiti, where governments are especially ³⁵ weak, and in politically unstable countries, like Iraq and Afghanistan. He says, "It's highly risky. Some of the aid is going to disappear. Some of it is going to be stolen. That is just the environment you are working in. I don't think that means that ⁴⁰ we don't take that risk. I do think it means that we need to be careful, that we take good opportunities and we do the best that we can. But sometimes, we are going to fail."

United Nations analysts acknowledge that ⁴⁵ foreign aid runs into difficulties in parts of the world that have little or no democratic infrastructure, such as Sub-Saharan Africa, where poverty levels have risen from 41 percent in 1981 to 46 percent in 2001. ⁵⁰

Long-Term Success

Nonetheless, Luca Barbone, Director of the World Bank's Poverty Reduction Program says foreign aid has contributed to an overall brighter global picture. ⁵⁵

Foreign and local aid workers take cover behind a truck as a humanitarian aid cargo plane takes off in Akuem village in southern Sudan. In Sudan and elsewhere across Africa, non-governmental organizations (NGOs) have built schools and boreholes for water, and provided health services and food for the needy. Critics say such outside intervention creates a culture of dependence that absolves African governments of their duties in a continent weakened by poverty, war, famine, AIDS and corruption.

(REUTERS/David Mwangi)

"If you look at the worldwide experience, there has been quite a substantial reduction in poverty levels as measured by income poverty over the last 20 years or so. So while it is true that in Sub-Saharan Africa there's been less than what is desirable, I think that the global numbers indicate quite a substantial success from the poverty point of view," says Mr. Barbone.

According to the World Bank, the number of people living in extreme poverty, on less than a dollar a day, has fallen by another 8 percent from 1.2 billion in 1990 to 1.1 billion people in 2001. But the World Bank's Luca Barbone says the international community has learned from past successes and failures how to use foreign aid more effectively.

Mr. Barbone adds, "The international community and the donor countries themselves have to give very high priority to having good systems of financial control and expenditure control in place. So I would say that the concern goes beyond the aid that is provided in the form of grants or loans. The concern goes really to the capacity of the country to utilize public monies in general, in a non-corrupt and effective manner."

Corruption and Foreign Aid Reliance

Because aid grants are often diverted to corrupt officials in undemocratic countries, some analysts are calling for a new approach. American University economist, George Ayitey, a native of Ghana, says new strategies are needed because foreign aid typically has failed, especially in Africa.

"If you look at the budgets of several African countries, Uganda for example, Uganda's budget is 53 percent aid dependent. And if you take a country like Ghana, Ghana's budget is almost 58 percent aid dependent. In other words, the recipient governments expect to get more aid from you in the future."

Professor Ayitey says the West should reduce the amount of foreign aid it donates and remove trade barriers, especially for the types of goods that developing countries are likely to export, such as agricultural products and textiles. But Mohamed Akhter, President of InterAction, an alliance of 165 non-governmental agencies and humanitarian organizations in Washington, D.C., says foreign aid can succeed if donor countries designate their monetary aid for specific purposes.

Mr. Akhter adds, "Health and education are two areas that take you out of poverty toward prosperity. And I can say this because I myself belong to a very poor family. It is only through education that one is able to break through the cycle of poverty. Second, you work with the governments to make sure that they have an infrastructure with less corruption, and that the aid they are given is appropriately utilized to help the people and not line their own pockets."

In an attempt to address the problems with foreign aid, 189 nations participating in the United Nations Millennium summit in September 2000 signed the Millennium Declaration, which paves the way for a massive effort to slash global poverty levels in half by 2015. But the goals outlined in the Declaration also recognize that, in order for foreign assistance to be more effective, countries receiving aid must invest in human capital, build democratic institutions, and respect human rights and the rule of law.

By Aida Akl Washington, D.C. 06 December 2005
Voice of America

d States 0.10
0.07
Long-Term
Nonetheless, Luca Barbone, Director of the
Bank's Poverty Reduction Program says
...d has contributed to an overall brighter

Words and Idioms

Vocabulary
Match each word to its definition.

1. ineffective *(adj)* ●
2. incompetent *(adj)* ●
3. rural *(adj)* ●
4. donor *(n)* ●
5. risky *(adj)* ●
6. infrastructure *(n)* ●
7. income *(n)* ●
8. substantial *(adj)* ●
9. priority *(n)* ●
10. expenditure *(n)* ●

11. utilize *(v)* ●
12. corrupt *(adj)* ●
13. budget *(n)* ●
14. textile *(n)* ●
15. alliance *(n)* ●
16. prosperity *(n)* ●
17. recognize *(v)* ●

● a. one who gives something to others
● b. significant; notable; large
● c. an amount of money spent on something
● d. having no ability; useless
● e. related to dishonest use of power
● f. a woven material; cloth
● g. not able to successfully complete a certain task
● h. wealth and/or material success
● i. to realize, admit, and acknowledge
● j. an agreement between countries or groups to work together to achieve a shared purpose
● k. from the countryside
● l. an amount of money allocated for a specific purpose
● m. a task or characteristic more important than others
● n. possibly unsafe
● o. to use something effectively
● p. the amount of money someone earns
● q. an organized system of communication and services

Idioms and Expressions
Fill in the blanks with the correct idiom or expression.

produce mixed results: when an action generates both negative and positive outcomes
My report card contained mixed results this year; I got As in math and science, but failed two language subjects.

a brighter picture: when something appears more positive or hopeful than before
I thought Granddad was dying, but Dr. Simons painted a brighter picture of his chances of surviving the cancer.

line one's own pockets: to become richer by dishonestly taking money intended to be used for other purposes
The dishonest employer lined his own pockets with company funds for years before he was fired.

1. My new boss painted _____ of my future with the company.

2. The officials _____ with the donations they collected from the public.

3. The fundraiser _____: we made money from the raffle, but suffered a loss on the bake sale.

Exploring Content

A. Complete the chart below.

Intended Benefits of Foreign Aid	Problems of Foreign Aid

B. Match the following people to their opinion.

1. Michael Radew   **a.** We do the best we can, but sometimes we fail.

2. Steve Radelet   **b.** New strategies are needed.

3. Luca Barbone   **c.** Foreign aid has contributed to an overall brighter global picture.

4. George Ayitey   **d.** Foreign aid is ineffective and may even be harmful.

5. Mohamed Akhter   **e.** We need to invest in health and education.

A Mixed Bag
Michael Radew, a Senior Fellow wit
in New York says re

Summary & Discussion

Summary
Fill in the blanks.

priority	infrastructure	rural	mixed results	donor
ineffectively	substantial	expenditure	incompetent	brighter picture

Economists are debating whether donating **1** _____ amounts of money to poorer nations is helpful in the long run. Most economists feel that, at best, aid has produced only **2** _____. Despite the fact that the **3** _____ should be to create **4** _____ such as roads, schools, and hospitals to help the education, health, and business sectors, what often happens is that **5** _____ and corrupt officials end up misusing or stealing the money. Another problem is that countries can become too dependent on foreign aid. Often, funds from **6** _____ nations end up being **7** _____ used, and this puts people in **8** _____ areas at a disadvantage. Some experts argue that, overall, foreign aid has produced a **9** _____ by reducing global poverty. They believe that rich nations should continue to do the best they can to help the poor. By monitoring foreign aid **10** _____, we can prevent its misuse and aim to provide support for poor countries so that they can eventually achieve economic empowerment and donate money to others in turn.

Discussion
Discuss these questions with your class.

1. If you were donating money for development in a poor country, what would you invest in?

2. How would you attempt to monitor how the money was spent?

3. Has your country ever received foreign aid? For what?

4. If you were very poor, what things would be most important to you?
Make a list in order of priority.

Safe Water

Warm-up

Can you drink water directly from the tap in your sink, or do you have to boil it first? The latter is true for billions of people in developing countries. Experts estimate that about three-and-a-half billion people lack clean drinking water and sanitation. The problem is not a lack of fresh water; it's a lack of proper infrastructure to provide fresh water. Already, nearly half of all the people in the developing world suffer from diseases caused by unsafe water and poor sanitation. The United Nations recently began a 10-year program to help change this situation. But is it already too late?

Points to Notice

Compare the concerns expressed by Erik Peterson and Claudia Sadoff with the solutions proposed by Susan Murcott. What potential consequences of a world water shortage does Mr. Peterson hint at?

Cultural Notes and Background

Citizens in developed countries such as the United States, Australia, and Japan take clean water and sanitation for granted. They are often appalled at the unsanitary conditions they encounter when traveling in developing nations. Many Americans do not drink water from mountain streams and rivers until they have put it through portable filters that eliminate contaminants and organisms, such as *giardia lamblia*. There are even parts of the U.S. in which it is unsafe to drink tap water as problems with parasitic organisms spread.

UN Effort Aims to Bring Safe Water to Billions

Indonesian environmental activists hold a poster as they stage a demonstration commemorating World Water Day near the water fountain of the main roundabout in Jakarta, Indonesia. The United Nations General Assembly designated March 22 each year as World Water Day to promote conservation and development of water resources.

(AP Photo/Tatan Syuflana)

March 22 marks the annual observance of U.N. World Water Day and the beginning of a U.N.-mandated decade of action called "Water for Life." They are a call to U.N. agencies and other groups to focus their efforts on reversing 5 *the plight of the billions of people who lack access to safe water and sanitation to protect their health. Organizers say the first water decade in the 1980s brought water to more than one billion people and sanitation to almost 770* 10 *million. But as VOA's David McAlary reports from Washington, the goal of sufficient safe water remains elusive as world population grows.*

Earth may be unique in the universe for its 15 abundance of water, amounting to 70 percent of its surface. But the image recalls the old sailor's lament, "Water, water everywhere, but not a drop to drink," for the vast majority of it is salty and unfit for consumption. 20

"It is really remarkable that on the blue planet, on a planet as abundant with water as the one on which we find ourselves, only three percent of the water resources on the planet are fresh water."

Erik Peterson of the Center for Strategic and 25 International Studies in Washington points out that as small an amount as three percent is, only a tiny fraction of that percentage is available to us for daily use. Most of the world's fresh water is either frozen, locked underground, or in swamps, 30 leaving less than a drop in every liter for our needs. Half of that is already in use for agriculture, industry, and cities and towns.

But about one-sixth of humanity, one billion people, do not have safe water and 2.5 billion are 35 without sanitation. U.N. statistics show that nearly half of all people in the developing world suffer diseases like cholera and diarrhea as a direct result. As the population grows, Mr. Peterson says more will be exposed. 40

"We believe that these problems, as daunting as they are, are going to become all the more daunting in the future," he said. "By current estimates from the United Nations, we believe that by the year 2025, some three billion people 45 across the world could face water shortages, in some cases life threatening water shortages."

Despite the minuscule amount of available fresh water, experts say there is enough to meet human needs. The real problem is that the 50 infrastructure to deliver it, such as sewage treatment plants and pipes, is lacking in many countries.

At the World Bank in Washington, Claudia Sadoff makes the distinction between physical 55 scarcity and economic scarcity.

"That is the issue, not so much of the resource not existing, but the resource being economically inaccessible," she said. "Forty-five percent of the world is essentially uncovered for water supply 60 and sanitation."

The outcome is that much labor that could otherwise be economically productive in poor countries is spent toting water long distances on foot from rivers and lakes. 65

Development and stability are affected as nations and regions within nations compete for this scarce resource.

India and Pakistan, for example, are seeking World Bank mediation over India's desire to 70 build a dam that Pakistan complains will reduce the water it gets from a river in Kashmir. Iran is building a huge dike that could divert some water it shares with Iraq.

Erik Peterson says water is a transboundary 75 issue in many places.

"Two-hundred-sixty water basins across the planet are shared by two or more countries. Thirteen are shared by five or more countries," he said. "How successfully these countries deal 80 with this critically short resource will, in effect, determine whether we have instability and conflict or whether we can define new pathways of cooperation going into the future."

In 2000, U.N. members set a goal of reducing 85 the percentage of people lacking clean water and sanitation by half as one of several so-called Millennium Development Goals to be met by 2015.

But the Center for Strategic and International Studies says the effort is underfunded and will 90 require an extra $15 to $30 billion in addition to the $30 billion already invested each year in development.

Experts say demand for water must be reduced as population increases. 95

For Massachusetts Institute of Technology engineer Susan Murcott, part of the answer is new technologies to increase water efficiency. She favors simple, inexpensive ones for poor countries, such as portable solar evaporation 100 stills to remove salt from water or drip lines connected to soil moisture sensors to release water sporadically onto farm fields as needed, rather than flooding them.

Ms. Murcott has developed a filter of brick 105 chips, rusty nails, sand, and gravel in a tub to eliminate arsenic and other contaminants from water.

An unidentified man collects water from a well in Kano, Northern Nigeria. As nations celebrate World Water Day, millions of people around the world, especially in developing countries, continue to face water shortages.

(AP Photo/George Osodi)

"There may be a movement maybe not away from centralized drinking water and wastewater 110 treatment plants," she noted, "but certainly an additional component of decentralized solutions that we are going to be seeing because water supply for so many people around the world is coming to people from decentralized sources." 115

To this end, the World Health Organization is collaborating with more than 200 governmental and non-governmental organizations, corporations, and universities in an international network to promote research into safe, affordable household 120 water treatment, and ways to make it available to every person who needs it.

By David McAlary Washington 17 March 2005
Voice of America

Vocabulary

Match each word to its definition.

1. mark *(v)* ●	● a. the cleanliness and safety of public facilities
2. mandate *(v)* ●	● b. difficult; challenging
3. plight *(n)* ●	● c. human waste carried off in pipes or drains
4. sanitation *(n)* ●	● d. a machine that distills (evaporates or separates) liquids
5. elusive *(adj)* ●	● e. to command; to order
6. abundant *(adj)* ●	● f. not controlled by a central source or authority
7. daunting *(adj)* ●	● g. a wall to hold back water
8. sewage *(n)* ●	● h. to single out or identify
9. mediation *(n)* ●	● i. easily carried or moved
10. dike *(n)* ●	● j. not occurring often or on a regular schedule
11. basin *(n)* ●	● k. hard to obtain or reach
12. portable *(adj)* ●	● l. to work together with others
13. still *(n)* ●	● m. to observe carefully; to notice
14. sporadically *(adv)* ●	● n. a difficult or bad situation
15. note *(v)* ●	● o. a region drained by a single river system
16. decentralized *(adj)* ●	● p. an attempt to solve differences between two parties
17. collaborate *(v)* ●	● q. easily obtainable; plentiful

Idioms and Expressions

Fill in the blanks with the correct idiom or expression.

point out: to call attention to something
He pointed out that, though half the water was gone, the glass was still half-full.

so-called: a name or term given by someone else, with which the author/speaker does not necessarily agree
The government did not honor its so-called peace treaties with the indigenous people.

to this end: toward this goal
It is important to recycle. To this end, we should always separate our garbage and take it to recycling centers.

1. Let me _____ the differences between an alligator and a crocodile.

2. _____, the students are planting trees to make the city greener.

3. They arrested the _____ spy on Wednesday.

Exploring Content

A. Complete the sentences based on the reading.

1. Susan Murcott believes that part of the answer for providing water to poor countries is _____.

2. Erik Peterson says that in many places water is _____.

3. Claudia Sadoff distinguishes between _____.

4. David McAlary reports that the goal of sufficient safe water _____ _____.

B. Choose the best answer.

1. What is the main idea of the article?
   a. The United Nations is mandating "Water for Life."
   b. Only a tiny fraction of the Earth's fresh water is available for daily human use.
   c. Unsafe drinking water causes diseases.
   d. Poor countries suffer because of limited access to fresh water.

2. What can be inferred about the United States?
   a. It uses most of the world's water.
   b. It has a strong infrastructure.
   c. It doesn't have good sanitation.
   d. All of its labor is economically productive.

3. Read the following sentence.

   "Forty-five percent of the world is essentially uncovered for water supply and sanitation."

   Which of the following sentences best expresses the essential information in the above sentence?
   a. Almost half the world suffers economic scarcity of clean water.
   b. Physical scarcity of water is a problem faced by close to half the world.
   c. Forty-five percent of the world has safe water and sanitation.
   d. Over half the world must live under inadequate sanitary conditions.

"It is really remarkable that on the
...as abundant with water a

Summary
Fill in the blanks.

portable	sanitation	decentralized	marked	abundant
sporadically	basins	point out	daunting	plight

The United Nations' 2006 "World Water Day" **1** _____ the start of the organization's decade-long project to improve the **2** _____ of billions of people who lack access to safe water and **3** _____. Though the Earth has **4** _____ water, only three percent of it is fresh water, and only a small fraction of that is available for daily use. Yet that is still enough to meet human needs, experts **5** _____. The problem is that developing countries lack the economic infrastructure to access safe water or provide proper sanitation. Also, countries are competing for resources in 260 shared water **6** _____. Experts project that these **7** _____ problems will get worse in the future. Massachusetts Institute of Technology engineer Susan Murcott says **8** _____ solutions are necessary, such as **9** _____ solar stills to remove salt from water, and drip lines that **10** _____ water farm fields. The World Health Organization is working with more than 200 international organizations to promote research into safe, affordable household water treatment.

Discussion
Discuss these questions with your class.

1. Where does your city/country get its water from?

2. Which water source or sources does your country share with another country?

3. What are some ways you can think of to reduce your personal water use?

4. What is the longest period you have had to live without easy access to water? How did this experience affect you?

World Population Growth

Warm-up

While the population of the world is growing rapidly, it is not growing at the same rate in all regions. Wealthier, more developed countries tend to have a declining birth rate, while the populations of poorer, still developing countries tend to be growing exponentially. The reason for the difference is that educated women in developed countries no longer want to have as many children as before. They also want to work instead of staying at home to raise children. In developing countries, lack of education and inadequate knowledge of birth control means people continue to have many children. The resulting problem is that more people are competing for fewer resources. In developed countries, the declining birth rate is also an issue; with an aging population and a declining labor force, economists predict there will not be enough young workers to care for the aged in the long run. The U.S. is the only exception to this trend.

Points to Notice

As you read, pay attention to the information and opinions associated with each of the following people:

• Michael Bowman — a broadcaster on Voice of America (VOA)
• Carl Haub — a senior demographer at the Population Reference Bureau in Washington
• Fama Hane Ba — Africa Director of the United Nation's Population Fund
• Elizabeth Chacko — a lecturer in Geography and South East Asia studies
• Nicholas Eberstadt — a demography expert at the American Enterprise Institute

Cultural Notes and Background

Demographics is the study of human development and movement patterns. Demographers study population growth or decline and things like urbanization, which means the movement of populations into cities. The work of demographers is very useful because we live in a world with limited resources such as food, water, and oil. The more people are born, the more thinly distributed the resources. At the same time, if the population declines too much, we will suffer a labor shortage because there will be no one to work in factories, run companies, or teach in schools. It is essential to find a balance. This is what demographers and economists try to help create, so that the Earth does not become overcrowded and or run out of precious natural resources.

World Population Growth to be Concentrated in Developing Nations

as Total Expected to Reach Nine Billion by 2050

By 2050, world population is projected to reach nine billion people. That would constitute a 38 percent jump from today's population total of 6.5 billion, and more than five times the 1.6 billion people believed to have existed in 1900. Demographers foresee declining, more aged populations in many industrialized nations and explosively growing, ever-younger populations in much of the developing world. VOA's Michael Bowman reports from Washington, both trends are seen as problematic.

If projections hold true, future global population growth will be heavily concentrated in Latin America, Africa, and South Asia. Carl Haub is senior demographer at the Washington-based Population Reference Bureau. "All world population growth today is in the developing world. There is no natural population growth in Europe, and even the U.S. is very heavily dependent on immigration," he said.

By 2050, Africa's population, both northern and sub-Saharan, is expected to surge from 900 million to almost two billion, while South Asia's population is projected to swell from 1.6 billion to nearly 2.5 billion. At the same time, Europe's population is expected to shrink from 730 million to 660 million.

Haub has sobering words for African governments worried about resource management in the face of explosive population growth, or European governments concerned about providing for an increasingly aged population: in the short-term, little can be done. "Demographic momentum is such that you cannot change something overnight. We cannot go back and have the babies we should have had in 1985. Whatever goal you

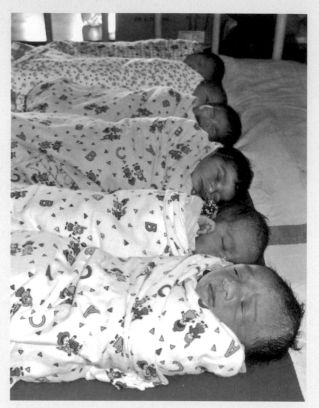

Newborn babies sleep in a maternity ward in Agartala, India. India is currently the second most populous country in the world, with a projected population of over 1.1 billion by 2010.

(AP Photo/Shrabani Deb)

might set, you have to start doing something about it about a generation ahead of time," he said.

The bottom line is that fertility rates will likely remain low in regions where babies are most-wanted from a public policy standpoint, and highest in many regions where poverty and hunger are already prevalent. The United Nations Population Fund's Africa Director, Fama Hane Ba, says many developing nations are struggling to provide for their current populations and could be overwhelmed by future demographic growth. "One of the consequences is the tremendous challenges to the countries, the governments, and the populations to take care and to provide [for] social services, to these growing populations, and also employment opportunities," she said.

Experts also foresee increased urbanization in the developing world. Elizabeth Chacko, who teaches geography and South Asia studies at George Washington University, comes from India, which is expected to account for one-fifth of world population growth over the next 50 years. "When you think about population growth at large, there is the density factor. People do not just spread evenly across the country. They are crowded in the cities, they are crowded in the coastal plains. And that makes for all kinds of problems. We know that with higher density there are often higher rates of crime, greater chance of the spread of epidemics," she said.

But Chacko notes that population growth can also generate a larger workforce and a bigger consumer base, both of which tend to propel economic growth.

At the Washington-based American Enterprise Institute, demography expert Nicholas Eberstadt warns that 50-year population projections can prove inaccurate, since they involve predicting the reproductive habits of a generation that has yet to be born. Nevertheless, to the extent that rapid population growth is anticipated in the developing world, he says it need not spell disaster for the poor. "In low-income areas, there is continuing population growth. Does that mean unemployable people, or does that mean a vibrant workforce? It depends an awful lot on the sorts of policies and institutional settings in which one finds oneself. That seems to me to be a good[sic] argument for getting policies right and institutions good, rather than trying to fine-tune the birthrate," he said.

Eberstadt makes a similar argument for industrialized nations, noting that efforts by European governments to promote higher birthrates have met with little success. "Inducing women to become — let's call them "baby ranchers" — is a very expensive proposition when women have alternative occupations in the paid labor force. Most Western European countries have tried to "talk up" the birth rate, and not surprisingly, that does not work too well," he said.

Chacko notes that many developing nations

A model displays underwear by Triumph International Japan in Tokyo, with characters that read, "stop the birth rate decline." The undergarment was created to increase awareness of the issue of a serious decline in Japan's population, the company said.

(REUTERS/Yuriko Nakao)

have programs to promote contraception. She says she sees a common thread in regions where those programs have proven most successful: the empowerment of women. "Kerala [state] in southern India has had one of the lowest fertility rates [in the country] and everything we know about Kerala suggests that the women in the state have a high status; they have been educated; they have been working for a long time. And research has shown that even a few years of education can have a great impact on fertility rates, because this is a woman who can read, who can understand the kind of birth control she might want to use — but also be empowered to use it," she said.

Among developed nations, the United States is an enigma. Unlike Europe, the U.S. population is expected to increase by one-third by 2050. Demographers note that the United States continues to receive a large number of immigrants, predominantly from Latin America, and that immigrants tend to have higher birthrates than the domestic population as a whole. They also note that higher standards of living allow many American women to successfully rear children on their own, and that American men generally share child rearing duties to a larger extent than their counterparts in other nations.

By Michael Bowman Washington 07 March 2006
Voice of America

Vocabulary
Match each word to its definition.

1. industrialized *(adj)* ●
2. trend *(n)* ●
3. surge *(n)* ●
4. shrink *(v)* ●
5. urbanization *(n)* ●
6. epidemic *(n)* ●
7. vibrant *(adj)* ●
8. fine tune *(v)* ●
9. birthrate *(n)* ●
10. alternative *(adj)* ●
11. contraception *(n)* ●
12. empowerment *(n)* ●
13. enigma *(n)* ●
14. domestic *(adj)* ●
15. rear (a child) *(v)* ●
16. immigrant *(n)* ●
17. predominantly *(adj)* ●

● a. a sudden, strong increase
● b. the situation of an infectious disease affecting many people across a wide area
● c. vigorous; full of energy
● d. different; instead of or in place of something
● e. mostly; for the most part
● f. to make small changes to something to improve or perfect it
● g. the equipping of a person or group with power
● h. a mystery; a puzzle
● i. a pattern; a habit
● j. to raise a child by giving them food, education, etc.
● k. related to a country with developed industry, or the production of machine-made goods in factories
● l. related to the home or local area
● m. the prevention of pregnancy by using certain tools, medicines, or practices
● n. to grow smaller; to diminish in size
● o. a person who has moved from one country to live in another
● p. the movement of people from rural areas to settlement in cities
● q. the number of births per year for every 1000 people in a specific place

Idioms and Expressions
Fill in the blanks with the correct idiom or expression.

a jump from: a substantial increase or change for the better
Eating dinner at a good restaurant is certainly a jump from eating at home.

spell disaster: to indicate very bad luck or great misfortune
The stormy weather spells disaster for our picnic.

talk up: to make something sound very attractive
I talked Sam up to Tracy so she would agree to go on a date with him.

1. Ryan really _____ that new Italian restaurant, but I thought it was terrible!

2. Janet and Eric's constant arguing _____ for their marriage.

3. Mark's English grade made _____ 60% to 80% when he began to study with a tutor.

Exploring Content

A. Complete the chart. Use information from the reading text as well as your own ideas.

Benefits of Urbanization	Drawbacks to Urbanization
_____	_____
_____	_____
_____	_____
_____	_____

B. Find the synonym in the reading.

1. Find a word in paragraph 1 that means **country**.

   _____

2. Find a word in paragraph 4 that means **worried**.

   _____

3. Find a word in paragraph 4 that means **aim**.

   _____

4. Find a word in paragraph 5 that means **common**.

   _____

5. Find a word in paragraph 9 that means **achievement**.

   _____

Summary
Fill in the blanks.

| industrialized | alternative | trends | contraception | surge |
| spell disaster | epidemics | shrink | empowerment | urbanization |

Demographers, the scientists who study population dynamics, have begun to notice
1 _____ in both developed and developing countries, both of which could
2 _____ for these parts of the world in different ways. In more **3** _____
countries, populations are declining because women have started using **4** _____.
If these populations **5** _____ too much in size, governments will have to find
6 _____ sources of labor in these regions to keep industries going. Developing
countries are experiencing a population **7** _____. There is not enough education
and **8** _____ of women, so they keep having children. This eventually leads to
9 _____, which in turn can lead to problems like high crime rates and
10 _____, which reduce the quality of life. Too many people are competing for the
same resources in the same place. Whether the world can survive this imbalance in
developed and developing countries will depend on the policies and programs instituted,
including continued education for women in all parts of the world.

Discussion
Discuss these questions with your class.

1. Is your country's population increasing or decreasing in size? Why?

2. How many children do you want to have? Why?

3. Would you prefer to live in a city or in the countryside? Why?

4. How would you solve the imbalance between population growth in developed and
developing countries?

Stereotypes

**Choose two adjectives
countries of your ow**

- punctual
- tolerant
- romantic
- respectf
- hard-w
- emoti

American

British

French

Japanese

Koreans   Brazilian

Saudi Arabians   Turkish   Au

my

Kosovo: Waiting for Independence

Warm-up

Throughout world history, new nations have formed when people within one country desire independence from another country. Sometimes, this transition is peaceful. Often, however, independence involves conflict; usually war. This is just as true today as it was thousands of years ago.

Points to Notice

Note the contrasting viewpoints in this article between the United States and the European Union. Pay close attention to the information and opinions associated with each of the following people:
• Robert Hand — a US advisor to Europe
• Nicholas Pano — a US historian
• Robert Hunter — a former US ambassador to Europe
• Ioannis Saratsis — a foreign affairs specialist

Cultural Notes and Background

Kosovo is a disputed area of land in Eastern Europe that once belonged to the former country of Yugoslavia. After war split Yugoslavia into several different countries in the 1990s, Kosovo became an autonomous region within one of those new countries: Serbia. Tensions between two Kosovar ethnic groups — Albanians and Serbians — erupted into wars between 1996 and 1999, after which the Kosovo region came under control of the United Nations. In February 2008, Kosovo declared independence from Serbia and announced the formation of a new country: the Republic of Kosovo. Thirty-seven countries recognize Kosovo's independence, including the United States but twenty-seven other countries, including Russia, do not. In addition, about twenty other countries, including China, remain neutral.

Charting Kosovo's Independence

Kosovo, the restive southern province of Serbia, which has been under international control for about a decade, intends to declare independence in the coming months. But any move toward full independence by Kosovo, which is dominated by a large ethnic-Albanian majority, will face strong opposition from Serbia and its historic ally, Russia, which can block Kosovo's admittance to the United Nations. 10

Supporters display a banner showing Russian prime minister Vladimir Putin, and Serbian prime minister Vojislav Kostunica, reading "Kosovo is Serbia," during Serbian nationalist prime minister Vojilsav Kostunica's coalition pre-election rally, in Belgrade's Republic Square on Thursday May 8, 2008.

(AP Photo/Srdjan Ilic)

Since the unraveling of Yugoslavia that began with a series of bloody conflicts in the early 1990s, the international community has maintained multiple peacekeeping missions and poured millions of dollars of economic aid 15 into stabilizing the once-wartorn Balkan area and set it on a path toward democracy and a free market economy. Most of the successor-states from the former Yugoslavia have made important strides and are now in the European 20 Union or seeking membership. But the region has one last unsettled issue: the political future of Serbia's breakaway province of Kosovo.

Kosovo has been under international trusteeship ever since NATO's 1999 air bombing 25 campaign, which ended a brutal Serbian effort to control the province's ethnic-Albanian majority and drove Serbia's security forces out of Kosovo. Although, technically, Kosovo is still part of Serbia, its ethnic-Albanian majority 30 overwhelmingly favors independence, which the Kosovo-Serb minority strongly rejects.

Eager to scale back its commitments in the region, and faced with the growing impatience of Kosovo's ethnic-Albanians, the international 35 community, last year, began mediation efforts. But months of talks on Kosovo's future ended in a stalemate.

Meanwhile, Russia has threatened to veto Kosovo's independence if it comes up for a vote 40 in the U.N. Security Council. Moscow and Belgrade are calling for further talks. But the United States and leading European states say negotiations are exhausted and the status quo is untenable. 45

"The one thing that cannot be defended is a call for further delay. It's counter-productive it's unlikely to lead anywhere and it can only create greater instability," says Robert Hand, a senior advisor on the US Commission on 50 Security and Cooperation in Europe. "We simply can't leave a situation where the status of Kosovo is just kept on hold indefinitely. The people there need to know what their future is and they deserve to know what their future is. 55 I think the United States understands that and it's pretty firm in its position of where Kosovo needs to go. I think it is not a question of where we want to see Kosovo go, it is a question of how do we get it there"?

Objections to Independence

Russia and Serbia say it would be against international law for Kosovo to declare independence, and for countries to recognize it without a Security Council resolution. Moscow argues that it would set a dangerous precedent for some of the fifty or so territorial disputes worldwide. But others point out that, unlike many others, Kosovo's case has been internationalized.

Some experts contend that Russia, while seeking to restore its world power status, has been flexing its muscles in places important to the West, including, Iran, the Caucasus, and now, Kosovo. According to Nicholas Pano, a historian at Western Illinois University, just as the US is standing by its promise to Kosovo, Russia feels strong enough to keep its promise to Serbia.

"It's going to be very difficult for these parties to back off. A lot of it is going to depend on the general atmospherics of the international situation. Are we going to enter into a new period of competitiveness between the United States and Russia? Are we going to return to power diplomacy? These imponderables, I think, are still not yet clear, but certainly could influence how this issue is ultimately resolved," says Pano.

While there is broad agreement that Kosovo will remain a contentious issue, most foreign policy experts note that it is unlikely to cause a major fissure in East-West relations. Robert Hunter, a senior advisor with the Washington-based RAND Corporation, who served as US Ambassador to NATO and the European Union during the Clinton administration in the mid-1990's, says, "Russia is not going to war over Kosovo. It is not going to fundamentally change its position in regard to working with the Americans and working with the Europeans. But, if you want to build a constructive European security, if you want to build constructive relations with the Russians in many of the trouble spots of the world, it is worth creating a broader framework within which these matters can be discussed," says Hunter. "But I wouldn't turn around and say, 'I'm sorry,' if Russia is upset by what Kosovo might do. You Kosovars had better not do it."

Western Efforts

The United States, Britain, and France have already stepped up their efforts to gather support from hesitant members of the European Union for bypassing the U.N. and recognizing a declaration of independence by Kosovar Albanians. In what some experts view as a first step toward an independent Kosovo, a European Union mission will shortly replace the current U.N. administration in the province.

Foreign affairs specialist Ioannis Saratsis, with the Hudson Institute, says the United States is eager to close the chapter on Kosovo. But he cautions that the province might not see much improvement without active US involvement. "The Europeans have a very bad track record in the Balkans in general, especially starting from the first Yugoslavian war. They might see Serbia as a chance to prove to the world that they can act with a unified voice, they can have a unified foreign policy. I am not very optimistic on the European Union doing a great job in Kosovo or in Serbia."

Saratsis adds if leading European states recognize an independent Kosovo, Serbia's relations with the EU are likely to suffer, leaving the region unsettled yet again. Still other analysts say over the past decade-and-a-half the European Union has helped usher in a period of calm and development in large parts of an area that has often been described as "the Balkan tinderbox."

By Jela De Franceschi Washington 09 January 2008
Voice of America

Vocabulary

Match each word to its definition.

1. restive *(adj)* ●	● a. to bring under control; make stable
2. ethnic *(adj)* ●	● b. disagreement in thought or viewpoint
3. ally *(n)* ●	● c. to make more violent or severe
4. stabilize *(v)* ●	● d. a connected series of military operations
5. campaign *(n)* ●	● e. a formal expression of opinion
6. exacerbate *(v)* ●	● f. to try and peacefully settle conflicts
7. mediate *(v)* ●	● g. likely to cause disagreement
8. veto *(v)* ●	● h. relating to people who share common racial traits
9. exhaust *(v)* ●	● i. unable to be defended
10. untenable *(adj)* ●	● j. resistant; stubborn
11. resolution *(n)* ●	● k. unable to be evaluated exactly
12. precedent *(n)* ●	● l. a country that agrees to support another
13. imponderable *(adj)* ●	● m. to discuss completely
14. contentious *(adj)* ●	● n. to officially prohibit or forbid
15. fissure *(n)* ●	● o. an example or model

Idioms and Expressions

Fill in the blanks with the correct idiom or expression.

state of limbo: a condition of uncertainty
The election was in a state of limbo as the votes were recounted.

track record: past performance
She has a great track record for being on time.

tinderbox: a place where conflict, such as war or violence, could start easily
In the 1960s, Mississippi was a tinderbox for racial unrest.

1. Israel is a _____ for religious disputes.

2. The mayor has a poor _____ when it comes to keeping promises.

3. His athletic career hung in a _____ after the knee injury.

Exploring Content

A. Complete the sentences based on the reading.

1. Serbia and Russia have the power to _____.

2. According to Robert Hand, what cannot be defended is _____.

3. Robert Hunter says that Russia is not _____.

4. Ioannis Saratsis is not optimistic about the European Union doing _____
_____.

B. Find the synonym in the reading.

1. Find a word in paragraph 1 that means **prevented**.

_____

2. Find a phrase in paragraph 4 that means **decrease**.

_____

3. Find a phrase in paragraph 5 that means **current situation**.

_____

4. Find a word in paragraph 8 that means **argue**.

_____

5. Find a word in paragraph 10 that means **split**.

_____

Summary & Discussion

Summary
Fill in the blanks.

ethnic	resolution	veto	exacerbate	campaign
stabilize	contentious	state of limbo	allies	restive

Almost a decade after a NATO bombing **1** _____ ended war in Yugoslavia, the fate of Kosovo remains in a **2** _____. This **3** _____ province of Serbia, which has been torn by **4** _____ tensions, recently declared independence, a **5** _____ move that threatens to **6** _____ relations between major countries, particularly the United States and Russia. Russia has threatened to **7** _____ any **8** _____ for independence that comes before the United Nations. The US and its **9** _____, however, doubt Russia will go to war over this issue, and say it's important to **10** _____ Kosovo so it can move forward.

Discussion
Discuss these questions with your class.

1. How much do you know about the history and break-up of Yugoslavia?

2. Which type of ethnic groups does your country have? Are there any contentious issues between them?

3. Why do people sometimes want independence from their ruling countries? What are some of the possible ways they can obtain it?

4. What do you think is the best solution for Kosovo? Why?

Egypt: Youth and Democracy

Warm-up

In Egypt, unemployment and other frustrations are motivating the youth of the country to stage demonstrations demanding a more democratic government. President Hosni Mubarak has held power for twenty-four years. According to democratic principles, this classifies Mubarak as a dictator, because he has not been elected by the citizens of Egypt in truly free and fair elections. Instead, serious irregularities occurred during the latest election, held in September 2005. The youth are at the heart of democratic movements all over the Middle East, but some youths are also disillusioned by politics and have grown apathetic. Can they really effect change in the predominantly Islamic Middle East through their protest action?

Points to Notice

As you read, pay attention to the information or opinions associated with the following people and organizations:

• Kifaya — political resistance organization in Egypt, meaning "enough"
• Youth For Change — a political off-shoot of Kifaya
• George Ishak — 67-year-old co-founder of Kifaya
• Ahmed Salah — 38-year-old head of Youth For Change
• Doaa El-Shami — 21-year-old Egyptian who works on a popular Islamic website

Cultural Notes and Background

The majority of Middle Eastern and northern African nations are Islamic. Islam is the religion founded by the prophet Mohammed in the 6th century A.D. The God of Islam is called Allah. Islam is both a religion and a system of laws. These laws are usually very rigid and socially repressive, allowing few democratic freedoms. The laws are especially tough on women, who must remain fully covered in public and may not hold certain jobs or own property. Many young people in Islamic countries wish for democratic change in their countries so that they too can enjoy social and civil freedoms.

Youth Seen as 'Heart' of Democracy Movement in Egypt

The youth population is growing rapidly across the Middle East, and, in many countries, it is a force for change. Huge crowds of mostly young people have taken to the streets in Egypt over the last year, demanding democracy. In a country where half of the population is under the age of 24, the demands of youth are becoming more important than ever. And the scenario is echoed in other countries in the region.

Over the last year, pro-democracy activists have staged hundreds of street protests like this one, demanding change. They shout slogans boldly criticizing President Hosni Mubarak, something nobody has ever dared to do here before. The loosely organized movement is known as Kifaya, the Arabic word for "enough."

President Mubarak has been in power for 24 years. That is longer than some of the protesters have been alive. Many of these demonstrations are led by people in their 20s and 30s. They are part of a Kifaya offshoot, known as Youth For Change, headed by 38-year-old Ahmed Salah.

"Older generations are always more conservative when it comes to action in the street," he says. "Let's say, Youth For Change has been the spearhead of the democracy movement now, when it comes to action."

It would not be accurate to say that Egypt's pro-democracy movement is entirely youth-based. Some of its leaders are in their 60s, and one is 85.

A protester speaks in front of a huge banner which reads, "Enough Corruption, Enough Repression" during a protest in Cairo, April 27, 2006. Thousands of Egyptian police sealed off the area around the High Court in central Cairo as two judges appeared before a disciplinary committee to face questioning about their criticism of the government.

(REUTERS/Goran Tomasevic)

But those older leaders acknowledge that much of the movement's energy comes from the youth.

"You know, because the young people . . . they are the heart of the movement," says George Ishak, 67, one of Kifaya's founders. "They are the heart of the movement."

Young people have been at the center of other protest movements around the Middle East for decades. For example, university students played a major role in the Iranian revolution of 1979. Young Iranians were also behind the push for change that brought reformist President Mohammed Khatamei to power in 1997.

But the promised reforms there never materialized. The movement lost steam. Many young Iranians grew disenchanted with politics, and a hard-liner was again elected president earlier this year.

In Egypt, not all youth are enthusiastically engaged in political struggle. Widespread unemployment and disillusionment about the political process have kept many young people away from the polls in this year's elections.

In September, President Mubarak faced other candidates on the ballot for the first time. But voter turnout remained low, and local human rights groups said there were some serious irregularities. The State Department called it one step in the march towards full democracy, but also urged continued reforms to ensure that future elections are more credible to the Egyptian people.

Ahmed Salah of Youth for Change acknowledges that many young people are either not interested in politics or are afraid of the consequences of speaking out. But, he says, in the current environment, apathy is becoming a luxury that fewer and fewer can afford. He sarcastically compares life in Egypt to the dystopian novels of George Orwell. [80] [85]

"We are supposed to be living in the best country in the world," he says. "We are having the best kind of freedom that anybody could enjoy, and we should be very thankful to our government and our popular, lovable dictator all the time. This is crazy! How could you just take it? Wouldn't you just get to a point where you have to say, "no", and you wouldn't care whether you live or die anymore, because you can't get a job anyway?" [90] [95]

Mr. Salah says many young people feel they have no future here anymore. That leaves them with few options. They can try to emigrate, and many do. They can join the street protests. Or they can just give up. [100]

Doaa El-Shami, 21, is working for a popular Islamic Web site, but she says she knows many people her age who are unemployed.

"It is a very big problem," she says. "There are lots of college graduates who cannot find a job, and are doing nothing but selling belts or handbags on the street." She also says a disturbing number of young people — frustrated, bored, and unable to find work — are idling their time away in cafés, and some are turning to drugs. [105] [110]

But the first thing she mentions when asked about being young in Egypt is marriage; specifically, that many young people cannot afford to get married. That is a common complaint. [115] [120]

Egyptian tradition requires a young man to buy and furnish an apartment for his new bride. But with so many young people out of work, and real estate prices climbing, that [125]

is often impossible.

Ahmed Salah from Youth For Change knows first hand. [130]

"The same thing happened to me," he said. "I was engaged, and I recently had my engagement broken, precisely because I couldn't afford what I had to do, and because I lost my job."

But rather than give up, drop out, or move, Mr. Salah and other members of Youth For Change have decided to stay and fight for change. He says it is partly a matter of self-preservation. [135]

"Also being, in most of our cases, unemployed, or having very, let's say, not very rewarding jobs, due to the condition of the country — this also gives us another motivation, because we want to have a place in this world," he says. "And, for us, it is a matter of life and death, because, if we continue the way we are as a country, we will never have a chance. Most of us will never be able even to get married or ever have families or children, because there is no way to do so." [140] [145]

Mr. Salah says the problems facing Egypt are far from unique in the Arab world. He says the Kifaya movement has inspired pro-democracy groups in other countries in the region, such as Tunisia and Yemen. [150]

"Even Libya, against the dictator they have, yeah, there was a Libya movement called Khalas ["finished"], which is like Kifaya," he says. "It's the same idea. Of course, it's working underground, not like us, because it's much worse over there regarding what Mr. Ghaddafi can do." [155] [160]

An Egyptian anti-government protestor attends a rally in Cairo September 7, 2005. Polling stations opened for Egypt's first presidential elections with President Hosni Mubarak expected to win a fifth six-year term as the leader of the Arab world's most populous nation.

(REUTERS/Mona Sharaf)

It may be years before the world knows whether Kifaya and Youth For Change will actually achieve their goal of a more democratic Egypt. But, if change comes, Mr. Salah believes, it will have a ripple effect throughout the region. [165] [170]

By Challiss McDonough Cairo
15 November 2005
Voice of America

Vocabulary
Match each word to its definition.

1. activist *(n)* ●   ● a. the leading force or cause in a movement
2. unemployment *(n)* ●   ● b. to come into being or existence; to become a material reality
3. protester *(n)* ●   ● c. to choose through a vote
4. spearhead *(n)* ●   ● d. related to a very negative state; opposite of utopian or "ideal"
5. accurate *(adj)* ●   ● e. a person who actively works towards achieving social or political change
6. youth-based *(adj)* ●   ● f. special; one of a kind; different from all others
7. major *(adj)* ●   ● g. the condition of being without work
8. materialize *(v)* ●   ● h. generated by young people
9. hard-liner *(n)* ●   ● i. to have enough money to buy something
10. elect *(v)* ●   ● j. to leave a home country in order to settle in another country
11. disillusionment *(n)* ● ● k. a person who publicly disagrees or argues against something
12. irregularity *(n)* ●   ● l. a lack of interest or concern
13. apathy *(n)* ●   ● m. the state of having lost faith or hope
14. dystopian *(adj)* ●   ● n. a person who sticks firmly to a strict set of rules or regulations
15. emigrate *(v)* ●   ● o. clear; true; correct
16. afford *(v)* ●   ● p. an event or action outside of normal rules and conventions
17. unique *(adj)* ●   ● q. the largest part; the most

Idioms and Expressions
Fill in the blanks with the correct idiom or expression.

the heart: the emotional centre or core of something; the source
Nelson Mandela was the heart of the anti-apartheid movement in South Africa.

lose steam: to lose strength, energy, or inspiration
The efforts to collect money for a new computer lost steam, so we've been forced to keep using the old one.

ripple effect: when one thing affects or causes many similar ones to occur
Sally's exercising has had a ripple effect; her entire family has joined the local gym.

1. What is at _____ of that new government reform?

2. John's smoking had a _____ and now the whole office is full of smokers.

3. I kept _____ during the race, so I must be getting out of shape.

Exploring Content

A. Two of the following statements are FALSE according to the passage. Check (✔) the FALSE statements.

1. ___ Egypt's pro-democracy movement is entirely youth-based.
2. ___ The pro-democracy movement lost steam in Iran because young Iranians became disillusioned with politics.
3. ___ Voter turnout in Egypt's latest elections was excellent.
4. ___ Marriage issues are a huge problem for Egyptian youth.

Rewrite the FALSE statements using information from the passage to make them TRUE.

a) _____

b) _____

B. Find the synonym in the reading.

1. In paragraph 1, a word that means **quickly**.

_____

2. In paragraph 3, a word that means **demonstrators**.

_____

3. In paragraph 7, a word that means **large** or **important**.

_____

4. In paragraph 9, a word that means **without work**.

_____

5. In paragraph 15, a word that means **doing nothing**.

_____

Summary
Fill in the blanks.

| the heart of | spearhead | youth-based | apathy | unemployment |
| hard-liner | disillusionment | ripple effect | emigrate | lost steam |

In Egypt, **1** _____ and other frustrations are motivating the youth of the country to stage demonstrations demanding greater democracy. This is because President Hosni Mubarak is a **2** _____ who they believe does not govern Egypt honestly and fairly. The **3** _____ of such political movements can be considered **4** _____ because young people are at **5** _____ these groups.

Unfortunately, there are also young people all over the Middle East who suffer from **6** _____ and **7** _____; they do not believe politics can change their lives. These youths may give up or **8** _____, abandoning their home countries, but many are choosing to stay and fight. Even though the democratic movements led by youth may have **9** _____ in some instances, in others, it may well end up causing a **10** _____ that brings democratic change to the entire region. Only time will tell.

Discussion
Discuss these questions with your class.

1. Is your country democratic? If yes, how so? If not, how so?

2. Has your country always been democratic or did the political system undergo change?

3. Are young people active in politics in your country? If so, how?

4. What are some problems faced by young people in your country?

"New Europe" Goes Global

Warm-up

From the end of World War II until the early 1990s, most countries in Central Europe were communist, meaning their governments controlled all aspects of their economies. However, with the end of the Cold War, and the demolition of the Berlin Wall, the situation has changed dramatically. Since that time, these countries have been transitioning to market-based economies. Now, businesses there are ready to compete with developed capitalist countries for profits in Eastern Europe and countries that were formerly part of the Soviet Union. Can they be successful?

Points to Notice

Pay attention to how Petr Kellner became wealthy. Compare his story with the opinion of economist Thomas Blutt Laursen of the World Bank. Also, note the terms *cultural ties* and *geographic proximity* in the article.

Cultural Notes and Background

"Old Europe" was dominated by the influence of the former Soviet Union. The "new Europe" includes countries that were formerly Soviet republics, such as Croatia and Slovakia, and a unified Germany. In addition, formerly communist countries such as Russia, Czechoslovakia, and Poland have begun changing to democratic governments and capitalist economies.

"New Europe" Goes Global

Companies in the former communist states of Central Europe are beginning to expand internationally as many now have the financial strength and management skills to tackle markets in the less developed parts of Eastern Europe and beyond.

The first Czech billionaire to appear on Forbes magazine's billionaire list is 41-year-old Petr Kellner, who got his start when the Prague government began privatizing state-owned companies in 1992. His small office supplies company received a million dollar bank loan to buy controlling interest in the country's largest insurer, which is now worth $2.7 billion. Since then, Kellner's company has invested in Kazakhstan and plans to expand to Ukraine and Russia.

Kellner is emblematic of a new generation of western-trained capitalists in Central Europe, which economically has been one of the world's best-performing regions during the last decade. While the average annual economic growth rate in Western Europe has remained at around two percent in recent years, many emerging European economies have been advancing at least twice as fast.

Many analysts agree that the countries of Central Europe have successfully mastered much of the difficult transition from a command economy to a free-market economy.

Honing Market Skills

Hugh Barnes of the Foreign Policy Centre in London points out that Poland, the Czech Republic, Hungary, and Slovakia spent a decade sharpening

People celebrate Poland entering the European Union during celebrations at Warsaw's Old Town May 1, 2004, as Poland becomes a new EU member along with nine other countries.

(AP Photo/Czarek Sokolowski)

their commercial skills before becoming members of the European Union in 2004.

"The competitiveness which Poland and the Czech Republic, for example, had to hone assiduously during the process of accession, meant that when they finally made it into the club, they were very well placed to develop exponentially," says Barnes and adds that E.U. accession and the accompanying infusion of western capital have further strengthened Central Europe's confidence and financial prowess. He says "new Europe's" captains of industry are increasingly eyeing profitable acquisitions in the Balkans and the former Soviet republics.

"[Capital] outflow to some extent is a sign of maturity in terms of an economy moving forward. I think it is very much a phenomenon, which we are seeing in the more robust economies of Central Europe: Poland, the Czech Republic, and others as well," says Barnes.

There has been a significant upsurge in annual direct foreign investments made by Central European companies in the last several years. From 2002 to 2004, for example, Czech firms increased their foreign investments from about $250 million to more than $800 million, while Polish and Hungarian foreign investments grew from a few hundred million to more than a billion dollars.

Investing in the Balkans

Thomas Blutt Laursen, a senior economist in the World Bank's Warsaw office, says Polish, Czech, and Hungarian companies are buying up banks, investing in energy and telecommunications, and setting up new companies and joint ventures throughout the Balkans.

"If you look at Hungary, the Hungarian gas company M.O.L. has invested significantly in Romania. There is also the O.T.P bank, which bought a major stake in a Serbian bank. Hungary's telecommunications acquired Bulgaria's telecommunications. Actually, if you look at Hungarian investments, they now own a third of the foreign investment stock in Macedonia, more than ten percent in Slovakia, five-to-seven percent in Croatia, Bulgaria, Romania, Serbia, and Montenegro. I am sure we will be seeing more of this in the years to come," says Laursen.

Some economists argue that many Central European companies have advantages over their western rivals when doing business in the "old East." Dalia Marin, professor of international economics at the University of Munich and a specialist for post-communist economic transition, adds that entrepreneurs from former Soviet-bloc countries often are considered more acceptable buyers of state assets in Eastern and Southern Europe.

"Part of the success story in entering these markets is the cultural ties. You understand each other; you can trust each other because you know the way to do business. A shared communist past and a shared transition period are very helpful in understanding these markets. I do believe these countries have an advantage because of these common ties in the past," says Marin.

Expanding into Foreign Markets

In addition, Professor Marin says West European companies often use their Central European subsidiaries to enter former Soviet-bloc markets because of their cultural ties and geographic proximity. For example, Germany's Volkswagen used its Czech subsidiary Skoda to start production lines in Bulgaria and Romania.

Companies in the new emerging European economies are trying to make inroads into Western markets as well. Polish investors, for instance, have purchased several faltering international businesses, such as Italy's biotech firm, CONDOMI, Singapore's pharmaceutical company, SciGen, and some 150 British Petroleum gas stations in Germany.

But many analysts warn that some Central European venture capitalists face fierce western

Evening traffic in the center of Warsaw, Poland.

(LEHTIKUVA/Jaakko Avikainen)

competition both financially and in terms of business know-how. Economist Thomas Blutt Laursen of the World Bank adds that "new Europe" is still far from acquiring all of the trappings of developed capitalism. He cautions that restructuring and privatization of some economic sectors have stalled and that the entitlement system inherited from the communist era has yet to be fully overhauled.

"There is a bit of a pause in terms of reforms in Poland, but also in Hungary and the Czech Republic. Major reforms have seen very little progress in recent years, and, I think, they face a critical challenge in the coming years of addressing their main public finance problems," says Laursen and adds that the jobless rate in Poland, for example, now stands at about 18 percent, while western financial ratings services have expressed concerns over, what they call, Hungary's unsustainable budget and trade deficits.

But most analysts point out that the Iron Curtain has been pulled down and that Central and Eastern Europe's trade and industry restructuring is heading in one direction — toward market-based economics and away from the socialist past.

By Jela De Franceschi Washington, D.C. 24 April 2006
Voice of America

Vocabulary
Match each word to its definition.

1. tackle *(v)* ●
2. billionaire *(n)* ●
3. privatize *(v)* ●
4. emblematic *(adj)* ●
5. emerge *(v)* ●
6. hone *(v)* ●
7. assiduously *(adv)* ●
8. accession *(n)* ●
9. exponentially *(adv)* ●
10. prowess *(n)* ●
11. eye *(v)* ●
12. specialist *(n)* ●
13. proximity *(n)* ●
14. subsidiary *(n)* ●
15. falter *(v)* ●
16. fierce *(adj)* ●
17. trappings *(n)* ●

● a. to change from public ownership to private ownership
● b. diligently; with constant effort and focus
● c. a person who is very skilled in a specific field
● d. a company owned by another company
● e. extremely rapidly
● f. a high level of skill or ability in a particular field
● g. to attempt to manage or handle a problem or issue
● h. the attainment of dignity or rank
● i. a small distance apart; a closeness
● j. to sharpen to a fine point; to improve
● k. the outward signs; the appearances
● l. ferocious; violent
● m. to become unsteady; to waver
● n. to come into the open; to grow
● o. to look at something with the intention of acquiring it
● p. representative; symbolic
● q. a person with a net worth of one billion dollars or more

Idioms and Expressions
Fill in the blanks with the correct idiom or expression.

captains of industry: influential business leaders
Bill Gates and Stephen Jobs are captains of the computer industry.

make inroads: to enter a market; to establish a presence
U.S. companies are trying to make inroads into China.

Iron Curtain: the invisible political, military, and ideological barrier existing between the Soviet Union and western Europe from 1945 until 1990
An Iron Curtain descended across Europe.

1. The _____ disappeared at the end of the Cold War.

2. We're _____ in the PC market.

3. _____ led the change from farms to factories.

Exploring Content

A. Read the statements. Find a sentence in the reading that supports the statement. Write it in the blank.

Example: Petr Kellner's company is expanding internationally.
Kellner's company has invested in Kazakhstan and plans to expand to Ukraine and Russia.

1. The economies of Central and Eastern Europe are growing more rapidly than those of Western Europe.

   _____

2. Central European companies are increasing their foreign investments.

   _____

3. The economies of countries in Central Europe are becoming more capitalistic.

   _____

4. Central European economies are still not as capitalistic as the economy of the U.S.

   _____

B. Find the synonym in the reading.

1. Find a word in paragraph 3 that means **growing**.

   _____

2. Find a word in paragraph 5 that means **improving**.

   _____

3. Find a phrase in paragraph 9 that means **forming**.

   _____

4. Find a phrase in paragraph 15 that means **experience**.

   _____

5. Find a word in paragraph 16 that means **extremely important**.

   _____

Summary
Fill in the blanks.

prowess	eyeing	billionaire	Iron Curtain	make inroads
emerging	to tackle	captains of industry	accession	honing

Ever since the **1** _____ lifted, companies in Central Europe have been **2** _____ their business skills as they prepared **3** _____ markets in the less developed areas of Eastern Europe. Czech **4** _____ Petr Kellner is representative of the new, western-trained, Central European **5** _____ who are expanding their businesses internationally. Bolstered by their **6** _____ to the European Union and growing business **7** _____, countries such as Poland and Kellner's Czech Republic are increasing their foreign investments. Businesses there are **8** _____ profitable investments in the Balkans and former Soviet republics, as well as looking to **9** _____ into traditional Western markets. Analysts caution, however, that these **10** _____ capitalist economies still lag behind developed capitalistic countries. No one can deny, however, that Central European countries are fast changing to market-based economies and away from their state-controlled past.

Discussion
Discuss these questions with your class.

1. How would you describe the economy your country has?

2. If you could make changes in your country's economy, what would they be? Why?

3. What are some strengths and weaknesses of capitalist and state-controlled economies?

4. How might cultural ties, geographic proximity, and a shared past help countries do business with each other? How might they hinder business?

Africa: Poverty, Politics, and Disease

Warm-up

In most of the world, common diseases can be prevented with vaccine shots, which immunize people against those diseases. In Africa, however, politics, poverty, and war have combined to make vaccinating people extraordinarily difficult. International organizations have spent a lot of money in Africa trying to fight polio and other diseases, especially AIDS. Despite these efforts, the diseases have continued to spread. Is the situation improving? Experts aren't sure.

Points to Notice

As you read, pay attention to the paths polio and AIDS have taken as they have spread from country to country in Africa. Look for the causes of this pattern. Also, note what these important people have to say:

- Patrick Bertrand — Spokesman for Massive Effort Campaign
- Paul Zeitz — Director of the Global AIDS Alliance
- Thabo Mbeki — President of South Africa
- Yoweri Museveni — President of Uganda

Cultural Notes and Background

In recent years, many African countries have been affected by civil wars. There have also been frequent wars between neighboring countries. As a result, governments are unstable, and they change rapidly. Meanwhile, countries in Northern Africa, such as Ethiopia, have suffered from severe drought. This has caused a shortage of food and led to mass starvation. Africa has several of the poorest countries in the world. People from other continents are trying to help by sending food, money, and workers.

Africa's Poverty, Politics Give Diseases Big Advantage

Many health experts say that Africa's poverty and politics are to blame for diseases that in most developed countries are easily preventable.

International health agencies set out more than two years ago on a $2 billion campaign to stamp out the global threat of polio, the world's largest-ever health initiative. They believed they could eradicate the virus by the end of this year.

Not any more. In Africa, which has most of the world's polio cases, politics and armed conflict have played a major role in stalling the polio eradication program.

In northern Nigeria, government officials suspended the polio program two years ago after rumors spread that the vaccine caused sterility and AIDS. Health workers sent in to vaccinate children were taunted or stoned.

Although Nigerian health authorities have resumed the eradication program, the damage was done. Polio rebounded in northern Nigeria and spread to at least 17 other countries that had been polio-free.

Sudan is one of them. The number of confirmed cases of polio-induced paralysis in Sudan soared to 54, a dramatic and dangerous rebound in a country that had eradicated the virus just four years ago. Experts on polio say paralysis of limbs occurs in only one in 200 cases, leading them to believe that at least another 10,000 Sudanese were most likely infected by the polio virus. This fear prompted several U.N. aid agencies to issue warnings that Sudan was in the midst of a massive outbreak.

From the point of view of health workers, Sudan is a major crossroads between Africa and the Middle East. It's also a country where internal conflicts have been raging for more than two decades, creating conditions favorable for infectious diseases such as polio, AIDS, and tuberculosis. The fighting has led to a mass movement of people and crowded, festering camps for refugees and internally displaced people, known as IDPs. And what little health care infrastructure there was has been destroyed during the years of conflict. Not only that, the lingering volatility of regions like Sudan's western Darfur make it difficult, and even dangerous, for polio immunization teams to spread out across the country.

One of the polio campaign's worst fears was realized this year when Yemen, just across the Red Sea from Sudan, reported more than 400 cases of polio infection, nearly half the world's total cases, says Dr. Faten Kamel, the World Health Organization's regional director for the polio eradication program in northern Africa.

"By genomic sequence, we can trace the origin of the virus. The situation in Nigeria and stopping of immunization activities by late 2003 due to unfounded rumors about the vaccine had a very bad effect on the whole region," she said. "The virus spread first throughout Nigeria, causing a lot of cases of paralysis, and then to other countries: from Nigeria to Chad, and then the virus spread inside Sudan, facilitated of course by the movement of populations, whether IDPs or returnees. And the virus moved with people from Sudan to Yemen."

A recent polio case was found in Ethiopia near the border with Somalia, raising fears that the virus might surface in a country that has no functioning government, much less a health care system.

The virus, which is spread mostly by feces, can lead to paralysis and death. It was eliminated from the developed world in the 1970s, but at least 300,000 cases remained in poorer countries.

In some ways, the polio eradication program, backed by the United Nations and the United States Centers for Disease Control, serves as a kind of template for other global health initiatives, including the campaign to fight AIDS, malaria, and tuberculosis.

Patrick Bertrand, a spokesman for a Paris-based program called Massive Effort Campaign against AIDS, TB, and Malaria in Africa, says fighting polio and these other diseases requires the full support of the people in regions where the diseases hit.

"This example of polio can be taken to other diseases," he said. "We know that, especially in TB or tuberculosis and HIV also, that mobilizing the community is key for the success of any health intervention. And I think that's one of the good results of this polio eradication campaign. I mean that when you involve the community at every level, you have more chances to have success."

Many health experts say there is a link between AIDS and armed conflict in Africa, where 40 million people are infected with HIV. Infection rates among Africa's armed forces are staggering. Nearly a quarter of Ugandan soldiers tested positive for HIV, which is low compared with the Malawian army's 75 percent, or Zimbabwe's estimated 80 percent. South Africa's army, one of the best-maintained on the continent, found recently that more than 20 percent of its troops are infected with HIV and has stopped accepting HIV-positive recruits.

Those statistics worry health workers fighting the spread of AIDS, partly because African troops are often used in United Nations and African Union peace operations, including missions in Sudan, Burundi, and the Democratic Republic of Congo. Their fear is that soldiers, sent in to protect vulnerable populations, are spreading the virus.

Paul Zeitz is the director for Global AIDS Alliance, a Washington-based non-governmental agency that helps African communities fight AIDS.

"There's clear evidence that armed conflict and HIV are interlinked," he explained. "From the African continent specifically, we know that when there are conflicts where local populations are displaced and refugee situations emerge, that those environments become strong environments for increasing HIV transmission.

"African militaries have high rates of HIV infection," continued Mr. Zeitz. "When they're in operations, there are problems at times where they get involved with sexual activity with local populations, with sex workers. Rape increases in those environments. We know time after time that that is leading to increased risk for HIV transmission."

The first massive outbreak of AIDS on this

An Afghan refugee returning from Pakistan holds her son as he receives a polio vaccination at the UNHRC office on the outskirts of Kabul, Afghanistan, Afghanistan is one of seven countries where polio remains endemic, although ongoing child vaccination programs by the Afghan ministry of health, the United Nations Children's Fund, and World Health Organization aim to eradicate the crippling disease.

(AP Photo/Emilio Morenatti)

continent was in southern Uganda during the 1970s, where the spread of AIDS coincided with a Tanzanian-backed rebel invasion that toppled that country's reviled dictator, Idi Amin.

The leader of that invasion, Yoweri Museveni, went on to become the country's president. He helped mobilize the country against AIDS in a campaign that became a model for other African nations. The country's HIV infection rates dropped from 30 percent a decade ago to about six percent today.

Mr. Zeitz says that most African leaders have shown a willingness to step up to the AIDS challenge, but that many African governments, being short of cash, have been unable to follow through on their pledges to combat AIDS.

"African presidents in 2001 committed to providing 15 percent of their national budget into the health sector, in part to respond to the crisis of AIDS, TB, and malaria, and very few African governments are actually doing that," he added.

Yet, other African leaders have been slow to acknowledge the AIDS virus. South Africa has more than five million people infected with HIV. Still, President Thabo Mbeki, who rarely talks about AIDS, has suggested that factors other than HIV cause the disease.

Recently, Uganda's President Museveni has started backpedaling on at least one aspect of his country's AIDS-fighting ABC platform - Abstinence; Be faithful; use Condoms. Critics say the Ugandan president is emphasizing abstinence and faithfulness-in-marriage programs, more in line with what many health experts see as a major shift in U.S. funding priorities for fighting AIDS in Africa.

But in Uganda, as in much of Africa, many women and girls are unable to choose when they want to have sex, or with whom. And many health workers say that, on much of the continent, even marriage is a risk factor for AIDS.

By Raymond Thibodeaux Nairobi 31 August 2005
Voice of America

Vocabulary
Match each word to its definition.

1. poverty (n) ● q
2. campaign (n) ● k
3. initiative (n) ● i
4. eradicate (v) ● m
5. vaccine (n) ● a
6. sterility (n) ● o
7. taunt (v) ● d
8. paralysis (n) ● p
9. rebound (v) ● g
10. festering (adj) ● b
11. volatility (n) ● j
12. immunization (n) ● f
13. feces (n) ● h
14. vulnerable (adj) ● n
15. reviled (adj) ● c   *I revil*
16. backpedal (v) ● l
17. abstinence (n) ● e

a. a type of medicine that helps prevent a specific disease
b. getting worse and worse
c. hated; disliked
d. to insult or challenge
e. the practice of not having sex
f. the act of administering medicine to prevent a disease
g. to retreat or withdraw from a position or attitude
h. the waste discharged through the bowels; dung
i. a plan of action; a program
j. the tendency to turn suddenly violent
k. an organized operation to accomplish a purpose
l. to reverse one's previous position
m. to end completely
n. not protected; easily affected or hurt
o. the condition of being unable to have children
p. the condition of being unable to move
q. the condition of being extremely poor

Idioms and Expressions
Fill in the blanks with the correct idiom or expression.

stamp out: to get rid of something; to cause something to stop
China is trying to stamp out corruption.

armed conflict: a fight with weapons; a war
The disagreement between nations could lead to armed conflict.

time after time: occurring repeatedly; happening over and over again
The park rangers warned visitors time after time of the dangers of feeding bears.

1. _Time after time_, drivers get into car accidents after the first snowfall of winter.

2. The teacher wants to _Stamp out_ cheating in her class.

3. _armed conflict_ has divided the region for several decades.

Exploring Content

A. Two of the following statements are FALSE according to the passage. Check (✔) the FALSE statements.

1. __ The polio virus spread from Sudan to Chad to Nigeria.

2. __ Nigeria stopped giving polio vaccinations in 2003 because of untrue rumors.

3. __ The first major outbreak of AIDS in Africa occurred in Tanzania.

4. __ The president of Uganda is de-emphasizing the use of condoms.

Rewrite the FALSE statements using information from the passage to make them TRUE.

1. _____

2. _____

B. Match the places and people on the left with the correct description on the right.

1. Sudan c

2. Yemen c

3. Patrick Bertrand e

4. Zimbabwe h

5. Paul Zeitz a

6. Thabo Mbeki d

a. says that African leaders want to fight AIDS

b. has the highest percentage of HIV-positive soldiers

c. eradicated polio four years ago

d. rarely talks about AIDS

e. believes in community mobilization

f. has almost half the world's polio case

like Sudan's western Darfur make it d
dangerous. for polio immunizati

Summary
Fill in the blanks.

stamp out	poverty	vulnerable	eradicate	sterility
rebounded	immunization	volatility	armed conflict	vaccine

Politics and **1** _____ have hindered international efforts to **2** _____ polio in Africa. In 2003, Nigeria stopped giving the polio **3** _____ because of rumors that it caused **4** _____ and AIDS. The disease **5** _____ in Nigeria, then spread to at least 17 other **6** _____ countries that had been polio-free. It has spread from Sudan to the Middle East through Yemen, which now has more than 400 cases of polio infection. An effective way to **7** _____ the spread of polio is to mobilize the community, as Uganda did against AIDS in the 1970s. However, the **8** _____ of Sudan and other African countries has made it difficult for polio **9** _____ teams to do their jobs. Largely due to **10** _____, AIDS has rebounded in Uganda, and soldiers are spreading the virus across the continent.

Discussion
Discuss these questions with your class.

1. What do you know about polio and AIDS?

2. What are some types of vaccines that people in your country receive?

3. How do you think people could fight diseases in Africa more effectively?

4. Is it important to help stop the spread of contagious diseases? Why?

China Waiting for Democracy

Warm-up

We often link a country's economic system with a certain political system. For example, in many minds, capitalism equals democracy. To Americans, it seems strange to have one without the other, yet that is exactly what is happening in China right now. Though the Chinese government has committed to capitalistic economic reforms, it retains tight communist-style political control. How does this system work? How much longer will it survive?

Points to Notice

The reading passage quotes three analysts:

• Bruce Bueno de Mesquita — Chairman of the Department of Politics at New York University
• Clyde Prestowitz — an author and President of the Economic Strategy Institute in Washington, D.C.
• Minxin Pei — Director of the China Program at the Carnegie Endowment for International Peace in Washington

What are the main points each of them make? How does their analysis complement the thesis of the passage?

Cultural Notes and Background

After the death of its initial leader, Mao Zedong, in 1976, China initiated a series of capitalist-style economic reforms aimed at opening its market to the outside world. Its leaders went cautiously, one step at a time. They were later influenced by the example of the former Soviet Union, which tried a futile simultaneous change to capitalism and American-style democracy after its communist government collapsed in the mid-1980s. Today, China has a free-market economy in many respects. The state, however, maintains control of many vital industries, as well as the stock market. Private ownership of land is still forbidden. While Chinese citizens enjoy greater personal freedoms than ever before, censors in Beijing monitor Internet use closely, and the government still persecutes those who dissent against socialism.

China Waiting for Democracy

Many analysts say China is disproving a long-standing assumption in the West that democracy follows economic liberalization. They say China's rapid economic growth has helped its communist regime bolster its political legitimacy and stalled much-needed democratic reforms in China.

Ever since Deng Xiaoping launched major economic liberalization in the late 1970s, inaugurating an era of extraordinary economic growth in China, many Western observers argued that political reform would follow.

Bruce Bueno de Mesquita, Chairman of the Department of Politics at New York University says the assumption that economic growth produces an educated, capitalist middle class that demands control over its own fate has not been the case in China. He points out, "When Deng announced his economic reforms, the standard view in the West was that China was quickly going to become a different, democratic kind of country. It's now 27 years since those reforms were put into place, and there is no evidence of any meaningful change in the way governance is done in China."

Professor Bueno de Mesquita adds that authoritarian governments around the world, including China's, are showing that they can reap the benefits of economic development while resisting any pressure to relax their power. He notes, "What a lot of autocrats have figured out is that prosperity can be a substitute for freedom and democracy, and that the big threat to them is not promoting economic growth, promoting good health care, having reasonably good literacy rates, because all of those things are beneficial to productivity. What is harmful to them is people having the right to freely assemble, a transparent government, a free press. It is very cheap to suppress those freedoms while promoting economic progress, so that people are fed and happy and don't worry so much about turning their governments out of power."

Stifling the Internet

According to some estimates, China is the world's second-largest economy, after the United States. Its robust economic expansion has been fueled mainly by foreign investment. An increasing number of foreign businesses are operating in China, which is often called the "workshop of the world." More than 44,000 foreign operations, worth about $60 billion, were set up last year alone.

U.S. businesses are especially attracted to China's technology market, the fastest growing in the world. There are an estimated 110 million Chinese Internet users and that number will likely skyrocket to 250 million by the end of the decade.

But China monitors its citizens' Internet activity, blocks information from websites, and frequently jails those who are accused of what it deems subversive cyber-action. And, high-tech giants like Microsoft, Google, Yahoo, and Cisco Systems have to comply with Chinese censorship laws in order to do business there. They have been vociferously accused of aiding Beijing's crackdown on dissent.

Clyde Prestowitz, President of the Economic Strategy Institute in Washington and author of the

Chinese Internet surfers at computer stations in an Internet café in Beijing, China. Internet companies facing hearings before angry U.S. lawmakers say they can't resist China's effort to censor the Web on their own. But industry analysts say that even if Washington tried to enforce free-speech standards, it would likely have little effect.

(REUTERS/Lucas Jackson)

book *Three Billion New Capitalists: The Great Shift of Wealth and Power to the East* says American corporations often are caught in situations beyond their control.

He argues, "When Congress passed legislation to bring China into the World Trade Organization and when Congress agreed to give China most favored nation treatment [i.e. most favored nation trading status], it was taking steps to encourage U.S. companies to do business with China. Everybody knew that we were not dealing with a democracy. Everybody knew that the Chinese leadership had different views about handling information than we did. The companies obviously see China as a big opportunity. And if they are not there, other competitors will be. But it does call into question the extent to which global companies can be co-opted by authoritarian governments."

The Globalization Game

After years of complaints by free speech and human rights advocates, the United States Congress is considering new rules to govern overseas operations of American Internet companies. But trade expert Clyde Prestowitz contends that loosening Beijing's grip on the way foreign corporations do business in China requires an international effort. He adds that pressure is building within China itself and notes that a number of high-level former Chinese officials recently urged President Hu Jintao to ease censorship.

Analyst Clyde Prestowitz says, "Because there are important people in China who understand the significance of freedom of speech, there is a lot of room for the U.S. and other Western and Asian figures — Koreans, Japanese, and others — to play a role as well. They can sit down and talk to the Chinese and say, 'We are playing this globalization game and here is how the game really has to be played.'"

Many observers argue that despite the regime's efforts to gain more legitimacy through economic success, pressure for democratic reform will only grow in China.

Minxin Pei, Director of the China Program at the Carnegie Endowment for International Peace in Washington, says there are powerful transformational trends underway. He contends, "Rapid economic growth is producing two things: enormous social strain and instability that will build up pressure for reform; and secondly, economic growth is creating the right conditions — a middle class, private property, and interconnectedness with the international community — that will, in the long run, be good for democracy."

"Foreign companies," says analyst Minxin Pei, "are further diminishing communist control in China. They compete," he says, "against a state-owned company, so they are reducing the strength of the state-owned economy. And that will weaken, in the long run, the Communist Party's monopoly over economic power. Second, they are bringing the best managerial practices, which emphasizes competition, open-mindedness, and meritocracy that again will increase pressure on the system to reform and create a much more liberal culture."

Many critics and defenders of the role Western business interests play in China agree that the country's eventual democratization is inevitable. They add that with China's joining of the global democratic movement, roughly two-thirds of the world's population could, for the first time, live in free societies grounded in universal democratic norms.

Chinese President Hu Jintao (r) waves to well-wishers after a keynote address at the opening ceremony for the Fortune Global Forum titled "China and the new Asian Century" in Beijing May 16, 2005. Hu said China would work hard to open up to the rest of the world and help foreign businesses to invest in what has become the world's fastest-growing major economy.

(REUTERS/Jason Lee)

By Jela De Franceschi Washington D.C. 24 February 2006

Voice of America

Words and Idioms

Vocabulary
Match each word to its definition.

1. analyst *(n)* ●	● a. to boost; to promote; to strengthen
2. liberalization *(n)* ●	● b. to grow or improve suddenly and greatly
3. bolster *(v)* ●	● c. a person who rules with unlimited authority
4. legitimacy *(n)* ●	● d. to take into a group; to absorb; to assimilate
5. authoritarian *(adj)* ●	● e. a person who examines and makes conclusions about an issue
6. autocrat *(n)* ●	● f. a forceful measure or disciplinary action against undesirable or illegal activity
7. transparent *(adj)* ●	● g. the state of having exclusive ownership, possession, or control of an industry
8. robust *(adj)* ●	● h. loudly or noisily protesting in an attention-getting manner
9. skyrocket *(v)* ●	● i. the process of becoming less restrained or controlled
10. subversive *(adj)* ●	● j. to lessen the authority or reputation of someone or something
11. crackdown *(n)* ●	● k. a system in which the talented are chosen and moved ahead on the basis of their achievement
12. vociferously *(adv)* ●	● l. having or showing vigor, strength, or firmness
13. co-opt *(v)* ●	● m. intended to overthrow or undermine a government or political system
14. diminish *(v)* ●	● n. incapable of being avoided or evaded
15. monopoly *(n)* ●	● o. the quality or state of being lawful, true, or real
16. meritocracy *(n)* ●	● p. characterized by an enforced, unquestioned obedience to authority, such as a dictatorship
17. inevitable *(adj)* ●	● q. not hidden; easily seen and monitored

Idioms and Expressions
Fill in the blanks with the correct idiom or expression.

reap the benefits: to gather or obtain beneficial results, as if harvesting a crop
The country's economy reaped the benefits of hosting the Olympics.

fueled by: given power, energy, or momentum by
The real estate developer was fueled by greed.

loosen someone's grip: to erode or diminish power or strict control
The Democrats are trying to loosen the Republicans' grip on the south.

1. We will help the president get reelected, then _____.

2. They finally _____ the boss's _____ on the company's vacation policy.

3. _____ emotion, the Chinese soccer team defeated Brazil in the semi-final match.

Exploring Content

A. Read the statements. Find a sentence in the reading that supports each statement. Write it in the blank.

Example: China has a large economy.
According to some estimates, China is the world's second-largest economy, after the United States.

1. Western countries have long assumed that economic prosperity in China would be followed by political change.

   _____

2. Authoritarian governments have learned that they can provide economic prosperity without losing their power.

   _____

3. Economic growth can lead to democracy.

   _____

4. China will likely become a democracy one day.

   _____

B. Choose the best answer.

1. What is the main idea of the article?
   a. Democracy is inevitable in China following economic reform.
   b. China's stunning economic growth has enabled its government to suppress the rights of its citizens.
   c. China has contradicted Western assumptions about the relationship between economic liberalization and democracy.
   d. International businesses play an important role in transforming China's political system.

2. What can be inferred about U.S. businesses?
   a. They are concerned with reforming China's political system.
   b. Their chief concern in China is making money.
   c. They will eventually transform China into a democracy.
   d. Their chief concern is appeasing Chinese leaders.

3. Read the following sentence.

   "Many observers argue that despite the regime's efforts to gain more legitimacy through economic success, pressure for democratic reform will only grow in China."

   Which of the following sentences best expresses the essential information in the above sentence?
   a. Many analysts believe that the efforts of Chinese leaders to suppress democracy through economic growth will backfire on them.
   b. Many analysts contend that Chinese citizens will overthrow the government.
   c. Many analysts agree that the Chinese government will ultimately succeed in its efforts to gain legitimacy.
   d. Many analysts think that China's economic success will decrease pressure for democratic reform.

Summary
Fill in the blanks.

monopoly	diminishing	robust	fueled by	liberalization
analysts	meritocracy	authoritarian	inevitable	reap the benefits

Political analysts in Western countries have held a long-standing assumption that economic
1 _____ will be followed closely by democratic political reforms, but China is proving
the **2** _____ wrong. Even though China boasts a **3** _____, capitalistic
economy, it remains under the tight rein of an **4** _____ government. China's leaders
have figured out that they can **5** _____ of economic development without loosening
their grip on power. Nonetheless, many analysts believe that democracy in China is
6 _____. They point out that China's economy is **7** _____ foreign business,
and that foreign companies are already **8** _____ communist control. These foreign
companies are competing against state-run companies, and therefore challenging the
government's **9** _____ on economic power. Their emphasis on competition, open-
mindedness, and **10** _____ will increase pressure on political leaders to reform
and create a more liberal culture.

Discussion
Discuss these questions with your class.

1. What types of economic reforms has your country undergone in your lifetime?

2. What effects have these economic reforms had upon your family?

3. In your opinion, how closely is a country's economy linked with its political system?

4. What do you think democracy will look like if it comes to China? Compare and contrast it
with democracy in other countries.

Cape Town Carnival

Warm-up

Every country has special festivals that celebrate some aspect of their culture or an event of historical significance. Over the years, two of these annual festivals — Mardi Gras in New Orleans and the Rio Di Janeiro Carnivale in Brazil — have become world famous. Could the Cape Town Minstrel Carnival be approaching that status?

Points to Notice

As you read, consider why the Minstrel Carnival began and how it has changed, especially in the past twenty years. Pay particular attention to the viewpoints of Kevin Momberg, a festival organizer.

Cultural Notes and Background

From 1948 through to 1994, black and white people in South Africa were separated by a legal system called Apartheid, which means "separateness" in the Afrikaan language. Under Apartheid, black and "colored" — or mixed race — people did not have the same legal rights as white people. They were encouraged to move out of large cites, such as Cape Town, back to one of ten designated "Black Homelands." Sometimes, they were forcibly relocated.
Apartheid ceased after peaceful negotiations from 1990 to 1993, followed by the election in 1994 of President Nelson Mandela, a black man and former Apartheid protestor, who had spent many years in jail. The lingering effects of Apartheid still affect South African society.

(EPA/Nic Bothma)

Historic Annual Cape Town Minstrel Carnival continues despite challenges

It's been happening on the second of January every year since the mid 1800's. A day traditionally known as "Tweede Nuwejaar" or "Second New Year". The festival dates back to the mid 1800's when white American minstrels visited the Cape with black painted faces and banjos.

The colored community of Cape Town — who themselves have just recently been emancipated from slavery – mimicked these performers. But in their case, they painted their faces white and sang merry, but sarcastic songs, often ridiculing their former masters. These days more than 10,000 brightly dressed, singing, dancing participants, take to the streets of Cape Town encouraged by thousands of cheering spectators who line the streets from early morning.

One of the traditions of the Carnival is the colors of the costumes worn by the different troupes. In the past, it was such a secret that participants were blindfolded when they went for fittings.

According to Kevin Momberg, from the *Cape Town Minstrels Carnival Association*, this has changed. "Yes, that was something some people did, but obviously that was some

South African members of the Cape Minstrel bands perform in the streets of Cape Town, South Africa on January 2, 2008. The annual parade celebrates the tradition, which dates back to the days of slavery when slaves were granted a holiday on this day each year.

(EPA/Nic Bothma)

years ago. Now, in the recent ten to fifteen years it is not happening any more. Nowadays, because there is such a lot of competition and so many teams, the colors become something that people fight for. They want to have those colors so they cut the costumes first."

Today, the historical roots of the carnival are all but forgotten. The Minstrel Carnival is more a celebration of life.

Recently, the City of Cape Town has changed the name of the festival from "Coon Carnival" to the "Minstrel Carnival" because the term "coon" has a derogatory connotation to some people.

Kevin Momberg says, "We accepted that because in [South Africa] when we became a democracy, we obviously had to become more politically correct in everything we speak and say to each other, and so people don't feel bad when you tell them something. So yes, we are still comfortable with that, although we still use the name in its Afrikaans form, "Kaapse Klopse," which is still well known but I think that will most probably, in a few years time, also fade out."

Under South Africa's all-white rule, or Apartheid, the Carnival faced enormous

A performer in the annual Cape Town Minstrel parade on January 2, 2008.

(EPA/Nic Bothma)

challenges. Segregation, forced removals, and discrimination, made the troupes and their performances more difficult to organize. The government often placed the best stadiums off-limits to the colored community and where the carnival was able to perform it had to do so in front of segregated audiences.

Now, in the "New South Africa," the government is lending its support to the carnival and Nelson Mandela himself presided over its opening in 1996. And with tourism quickly becoming a pillar of the local community, city officials talk about turning the "Minstrel Carnival" into a celebration that will rival festivals in New Orleans and Rio de Janeiro.

Surprisingly, it's not a move welcomed by all. Kevin Momberg says, "Maybe I don't agree totally with that. Money is always a problem . . . If you come to our stadiums and we have got 10,000 people, if there is 500 white people that's a lot. So, it's the colored people that are practicing and I'm not putting a name to it, I don't have a problem with that. It is the disadvantaged people playing for the disadvantaged people. The tourist is not relevant where we are concerned, because they just come and watch. We don't have the statistics as to how many beds they fill up, how many rooms they book and what they buy. We don't get anything from that."

There are always challenges facing the Carnival, mostly financial, but somehow this tradition has survived for more than a century. And as usual, earlier this year thousands of minstrels took to the streets in a dazzling display of colorful satin uniforms, shiny parasols, painted faces, foot-tapping banjo tunes and dozens of brass bands, merrily blaring a cacophony of festive tunes across the streets of Cape Town.

By Marinda Claasen Cape Town, South Africa
11 January 2008
Voice of America

Words and Idioms

Vocabulary
Match each word to its definition.

1. minstrel *(n)* ● n
2. carnival *(n)* ● k
3. thrive *(v)* ● d
4. emancipate *(v)* ● h
5. mimic *(n)* ● o
6. sarcastic *(adj)* ● a
7. chide *(v)* ● L
8. troupe *(n)* ● e
9. root *(n)* ● b
10. derogatory *(adj)* ● m
11. segregation *(n)* ● C
12. discrimination *(n)* ● g
13. preside *(v)* ● j
14. rival *(v)* ● f
15. parasol *(n)* ● i

- a. expresses irony or bitterness through humor
- b. beginning; origin
- c. state of racial separation
- d. to grow and flourish
- e. a group of theatrical performers
- f. to compete with
- g. an act of prejudice based on race
- h. to free from slavery or captivity
- i. small umbrella
- j. to exercise control or guidance
- k. celebration with music, feasting, masquerading
- l. to reproach or scorn
- m. disparaging
- n. referring to performers who mimic other races
- o. to imitate

Idioms and Expressions
Fill in the blanks with the correct idiom or expression.

take to the streets: to initiate action
The president has taken to the streets with his campaign to raise social awareness.

politically correct: conforming to socially acceptable boundaries
It is politically correct these days to refer to Native Americans as First Nations People.

pillar of . . . : an essential, foundational part
The church has been a pillar of the small town for 200 years.

1. Founder Bill Gates has been a ___pillar of___ Microsoft for nearly three decades.

2. The protestors ___take to the street___ in their battle against global warming.

3. It is ___politically correct___ in America to use the title, Ms., for all women.

Exploring Content

A. Read the statements. Find a sentence in the reading that supports the statement. Write it in the blank.

1. The Cape Town Minstrel Carnival was inspired by Americans.

   _____

2. The history of the carnival does not matter much anymore.

   _____

3. Government leaders want to use the carnival to promote tourism.

   _____

4. Some people believe that tourists won't have a significant effect on the carnival.

   _____

B. Choose the best answer.

1. What is the main idea of the article?
   a. The Cape Town Minstrel Carnival has a long, colorful history and a bright, promising future.
   b. The Cape Town Minstrel Carnival has become one of the three largest carnivals in the world, and tourists flock to it annually from all over the world.
   c. The Cape Town Minstrel Carnival began as a festival in which blacks mimicked whites, but has been transformed into a festival in which whites mimic blacks.
   d. The Cape Town Minstrel Carnival has survived numerous challenges in the past, and continues to thrive despite new challenges.

2. What can be inferred from the reading about the government's opinion of the carnival under Apartheid?
   a. It thought the carnival should be bigger, and promoted it heavily.
   b. It didn't like the carnival, and tried to repress it.
   c. It viewed the carnival as an important tourist attraction.
   d. It had ambivalent feelings about the carnival.

3. Read the following sentence:

   "The government often placed the best stadiums off-limits to the colored community and where the carnival was able to perform it had to do so in front of segregated audiences."

   Which of the following sentences best expresses the essential information in the above sentence?
   a. In the past, carnival participants performed in big stadiums in front of diverse audiences.
   b. The government segregates the audience for the carnival, so that only black and colored people can watch the performers in small stadiums.
   c. The government used to prohibit black and colored people from larger stadiums, which forced the carnival to smaller venues and limited the audience largely to the colored community.
   d. The carnival was previously unable to be performed, until the government acted to segregate large stadiums.

Summary & Discussion

Summary
Fill in the blanks.

| mimic | rival | a pillar of | | parasols | Minstrel |
| segregation | troupes | politically correct | | thrives | take to the streets |

The Cape Town **1** _____ Carnival, which began as a forum for colored people to

2 _____ the ruling white class, **3** _____ today as a celebration of life. Each

year, thousands of costumed performers **4** _____ for a dazzling display of music and

merry-making that has become **5** _____ South Africa's second-largest city.

6 _____ of brightly-colored performers merge with shiny **7** _____,

painted faces, and foot-tapping banjo tunes in a festival that could soon **8** _____

Carnivale Rio and Mardi Gras on the world stage. The Minstrel Carnival has survived the

challenges of **9** _____, and faces new challenges as an old-fashioned art form

in a **10** _____ world.

Discussion
Discuss these questions with your class.

1. Why do you think festivals such as Mardi Gras, Carnivale Rio, and the Cape Town Minstrel
   Carnival are so popular?

2. Which festivals in your country most resemble the Minstrel Carnival? What are the similarities
   and differences?

3. How has that festival, and/or other festivals in your country, changed over time?
   Why have they changed?

4. What are some of the challenges involved with racial humor and mimicking in an increasingly
   diverse world? Is there still room for the minstrel art form?

America's Changing Family

Warm-up

To Americans, the word "family" has traditionally meant a husband, wife, and one or more children. However, what if something happens to alter these roles? Over the past half-century, the makeup of American families has been dramatically altered. There are more single parents than ever before. Couples are increasingly choosing not to have children. Furthermore, couples sharing the same living quarters are not necessarily husband and wife. As the number of households with traditional families continues to shrink, what effects will it have? How will the government react to these changing demographics?

Points to Notice

As you read, consider what has caused the change in American households. Pay attention to the opinions of Peter Francese, a New York demographer, and Peter Fagan, from the Heritage Foundation in Washington, D.C. Also, compare the opinion of Jennifer Gaboury with the President's proposed "Healthy Marriage Initiative."

Cultural Notes and Background

In 1970, 72 percent of the U.S. population was married. By 2002, it was only 59 percent, and there were 5.5 million unmarried couples living together. In the same period, the American divorce rate soared. Today, the U..S Census Bureau estimates that about 43 percent of all new marriages will end in separation or divorce. Another trend that has affected American families is the continual rise in the rate of women entering the labor force. In 1960, only 28 percent of American women had jobs. By 2000, it was nearly 60 percent, thanks in large part to legislation in the 1960s and early 1970s that banned sex discrimination in hiring practices.

Reading

America's Changing Family

Paula Jones holds her two-year-old son at a news Conference in 1999. Appearing on CNN's "Larry King Live" in 2000, she said financial obligations as a single mother with a looming tax bill and two young sons were major considerations that led her to take a nude assignment with Penthouse magazine.

(AP Photo/Mike Wintroath)

For the first time in the nation's history, fewer than 25 percent of American households are made up of a married man and woman with children.

In a recent study of American households, the United States Census Bureau found more individuals living alone or with a partner without children in 2000 than in 1990. Most of those living alone are widowers, divorcees, and elderly people. According to the report, people living alone comprised more than 27 million households in 2000, up from about 22 million in 1990.

Frank Hobbs, a demographer who helped prepare the study, says fewer Americans are living within what's often called the traditional family — a husband, wife, and child or children.

"Those households that are most common, if we talk about specifics are: Number one is living alone. It's more common than any other at 26 percent of all US households. A household consisting of only a householder, a spouse, and a child is actually in 2000 the second most common with 22 percent of all households. And the third most common consists of just a householder and a spouse, with no one else present."

Women and the Single Household

Many analysts say more Americans are increasingly living alone due to a variety of reasons that include divorce and economic and social changes that began in the 1960s. Peter Francese, a demographer with the Ogilvy & Mather advertising agency in New York, says the shift toward living alone is largely due to the economic and social gains women have made in recent decades.

"The story of the change in American households over the last 30 years is the story of the growing economic power of women, their ability to get good jobs, and to support themselves and their children without a husband. That is the most important change over the past 30 years and really describes the 'why' of so much of this household change."

The Cost of Marriage

In addition, Mr. Francese says so-called "marriage penalties" that levy higher income taxes on married couples also dissuade people from getting married. He adds many married couples are not eligible for the same benefits under current welfare programs for the poor.

Even though Congress recently passed a law that temporarily suspends the marriage tax penalty, Peter Fagan, a culture and family issues fellow at The Heritage Foundation in Washington, says the legislation benefits only the middle class. "The marriage tax has been reduced and almost pretty much eliminated for the middle class. But it is massive; it's draconian on the poor. And they don't pay taxes. So where's the marriage tax? It comes in the welfare payments. If you are on welfare and you cohabitate with somebody, you'll receive much more in welfare payments. If the same couple gets married, depending on the state they're in, the welfare payment will be reduced by up to 25 percent."

Moreover, Mr. Fagan says the demographic shift toward unmarried households, especially cohabitation, is becoming increasingly the norm. He adds, "There's been an acceptance of it, whereas it was seriously frowned on and lots of social effort was put into keeping families together before 1950. Particularly since the sexual revolution in the mid-1960s, splitting and setting up families without a married father and mother has become widely accepted."

Some analysts warn that children living with single or divorced mothers, or cohabiting partners are more likely to become involved in drugs and crime, and do poorly in school. Although others say many factors, including good health, parental guidance, and financial stability of a household contribute to the welfare of children regardless of the type of families they grow up in.

Jennifer Gaboury, a board member for the Alternatives to Marriage Project, an advocacy group for unmarried people, argues that there is no direct correlation between marital status of a household and whether or not a child is successful in life. She says that 12 million single parents in the United States are successfully raising children on their own.

New Realities, New Households

Because there are different types of living structures in the United States, including divorced parents and unmarried siblings raising their children together, Jennifer Gaboury says government policies should take into account the variety of households. She goes on to say, "There are a myriad of different designs of families, so we can no longer pretend that families come with a mother, a father, and several children. And we

According to the U.S. Census Bureau, the most common living arrangement of American households is individuals living alone.

(AP Photo/Mike Wintroath)

need to acknowledge that reality and support all different kinds of families."

The Bush Administration has proposed a new initiative to help strengthen the institution of marriage.

According to Bridgette Maher of the Family Research Council in Washington, DC, President Bush's program is included in welfare reform legislation, currently under review by the US Congress. She says, "The President's 'Healthy Marriage Initiative' includes allocating about 300 million dollars for marriage-strengthening programs. These can include premarital education classes to help people prepare for marriage or marriage strengthening classes which would teach couples how to better their communication skills."

Most analysts expect a further decline in the number of married couples with children during the next decade to one out of every five households. Because of that, some experts contend that federal legislation needs to catch up with the move away from traditional families, and extend tax and welfare benefits to single and unmarried couples that account for much of this demographic shift in the United States.

By Aida Akl Washington, D.C. 02 December 2005
Voice of America

e a nude assignment with...

(AP Photo/Mike Wintroath)

most important change over the past...
really describes the 'why' of so much of
...usehold change."

Words and Idioms

Vocabulary
Match each word to its definition.

1. household (n) ●
2. census (n) ●
3. widower (n) ●

4. comprise (v) ●
5. demographer (n) ●
6. levy (v) ●
7. dissuade (v) ●
8. legislation (n) ●
9. draconian (adj) ●
10. cohabitate (v) ●
11. norm (n) ●
12. advocacy (n) ●
13. correlation (n) ●
14. sibling (n) ●
15. myriad (n) ●
16. institution (n) ●
17. allocate (v) ●

● a. a type of relationship
● b. an established custom, practice, or system
● c. a person who studies demographics (the characteristics of human population segments)
● d. a man whose wife has died
● e. to discourage
● f. to live together as spouses, especially when not legally married
● g. a group of people living together in a single dwelling
● h. argument in favor of a cause or policy
● i. to impose
● j. exceedingly harsh; very severe
● k. a law or government rule
● l. a vast number
● m. to distribute
● n. the normal situation; the usual
● o. to consist of; to be made up of
● p. an official population count
● q. a brother or sister

Idioms and Expressions
Fill in the blanks with the correct idiom or expression.

frown on: to disapprove of
The company frowns on employees dating each other.

marital status: one's condition or state relating to marriage
John's marital status is divorced.

catch up with (something): to get up-to-date; to attain the advanced level or degree of another
Get a mobile phone and catch up with the 21ˢᵗ century!

1. Public displays of affection are _____ in some countries.

2. I _____ my son by learning how to operate an MP3 player.

3. She's only eighteen years old. Her _____ is "single."

Exploring Content

A. Two of the following statements are FALSE according to the passage. Check (✔) the FALSE statements.

1. __ The number of U.S. married couples with children is expected to drop during the next decade.
2. __ Peter Fagan says that suspension of the marriage tax penalty benefits the poor.
3. __ Peter Francese contends that the declining economic power of women is a major cause of household change.
4. __ People living alone comprise the most common type of U.S. household.

Rewrite the FALSE statements using information from the passage to make them TRUE.

a) _____

b) _____

B. Choose the best answer.

1. Which of the following best expresses the main idea of the article?
   a. Most people in the United States are now living alone.
   b. The growing economic power of American women has produced dramatic changes.
   c. America is moving away from the traditional family and toward unmarried households.
   d. U.S. marriage tax penalties have caused the breakup of traditional families.

2. What can be inferred about the Bush Administration?
   a. It favors increased financial aid for divorced people.
   b. It values traditional families.
   c. It has a deep concern for poor people.
   d. It is trying to support all kinds of different families.

3. Read the following sentence:

   "Jennifer Gaboury, a board member for the Alternatives to Marriage Project, an advocacy group for unmarried people, argues that there is no direct correlation between marital status of a household and whether or not a child is successful in life."

   Which of the following sentences best expresses the essential information in the above sentence?
   a. Children with married parents are usually more highly educated.
   b. There is a cause-effect relationship between failure and divorce.
   c. Household marital status is a key factor in determining children's future success.
   d. Children from married and unmarried households can be equally successful.

Summary
Fill in the blanks.

advocacy	census	cohabitate	households	levies
correlation	comprised	marital status	norm	frowned on

The traditional American family — **1** _____ of a husband, wife, and children — is in decline. According to the 2000 U.S. **2** _____, this type of family structure accounts for less than 25 percent of American **3** _____. In fact, people living alone are increasingly becoming the **4** _____. There are 12 million single parents, and many couples who **5** _____ are unmarried or without children. Analysts say one reason for this demographic shift is the growing economic power of women. Another is the "marriage tax," which **6** _____ higher income taxes on married couples. Non-traditional family structures used to be **7** _____, because it was thought that children of single or cohabitating parents would be unsuccessful. But Jennifer Gaboury, a member of an **8** _____ group for unmarried people, argues that there is no direct **9** _____ between a child's success and the **10** _____ of that child's household. Because analysts predict a further decline in the number of traditional households, they say the government should extend tax and welfare benefits to single people and unmarried couples.

Discussion
Discuss these questions with your class.

1. What type of household is most common in your country?

2. Has the traditional family structure in your country changed over the past decade? If so, how?

3. Do you know anyone from a single-parent family? How is his or her family life different from yours?

4. What do you think of couples living together without being married? Should they receive the same treatment as married couples?

Populations Aging Worldwide

Warm-up

Does it ever seem like there are a lot of old people in your city? Well, there are, and there will be even more in the years to come. All over the world, people are living longer and longer. How will this affect us? What changes will societies need to make in order to accommodate older people?

Points to Notice

Note what the following people have to say about the future:

• Richard Katz — editor of *The Oriental Economist Report*
• Ronald Lee — a demographer at the University of California
• Joseph Chamie — a research director for migration studies
• William Butz — president of the Population Reference Bureau

What question does Richard Katz ask? Is it answered in the passage?

Cultural Notes and Background

Societies with different cultures struggle in different ways to care for their elderly. In the United States, the government gives money to retired workers in the form of social security. However, this often isn't enough for retirees to live on; they must supplement it with their own investments and insurance. In China and most Asian cultures, children bear the responsibility of caring for their elderly parents. As those societies change, however, it is becoming more and more difficult for children to care for parents as well as their own families, especially since the implementation of the one-child policy in China. As people live longer lives than ever before, the entire world is affected.

Populations are Aging Worldwide

This century, the world is expected to experience an unprecedented aging of the human population in countries worldwide. Analysts predict significant implications for economic growth and the well-being of societies. 5

99-year-old Jim Corringe, right, embraces his new wife Dinah, 85, at the St. James Old Folks Home in Christchurch, New Zealand. Good friends for many years, the couple, each with three previous partners, now all deceased, are planning a honeymoon.

(AP Photo/Fotopress, John McCombe)

Developed World Graying Fastest

Demographers predict that by mid-century, people age 65 and over will compose about 15 percent of the world's population, up from about seven percent today. Aging populations are 10 growing especially fast in developed countries.

"Japan has got one of the most severe cases of aging of any of the industrialized countries," says Richard Katz, the New York based editor of *The Oriental Economist Report*, a monthly newsletter 15 on Japan. "In the current year, about 20 percent of the population is over 65, and half of those people over 65 are actually over 75. And the portion of the population which is over 65 is going to keep rising," says Mr. Katz. "It will be 23 20 percent by 2010, 26 percent by 2015, and almost 30 percent by 2025."

While Japan and most of Europe have the fastest growing elderly populations, the number of people over 65 is also on the rise in the 25 developing world. According to United Nations projections, that segment of the world's population will triple by the end of the century.

William Butz, President of the Population Reference Bureau, a research organization here 30 in Washington, says population aging is a result of declining fertility rates and increasing longevity. "The Chinese population is definitely aging because their numbers of birth have been relatively small now for decades. But it isn't just 35 China," says Mr. Butz. "The U.S., all of Western Europe, other countries with relatively low fertility rates, [such as] Thailand — you could also include South Korea and certainly Japan — are aging. In many parts of Africa, life expectancy 40 is also going up."

Demographers generally agree that population aging represents a "success story," with increasing numbers of people worldwide enjoying longer lives. For example, according to U.N. demographic 45 projections, a child born today can expect to live, on average, until the age of 65. Half-a-century ago, life expectancy at birth was less than 50 years. However, analysts such as Richard Katz also note the sustained increase in the number of older 50 people — usually defined as persons over the age of 65 — poses many challenges to their societies.

"How are you going to support the retirees? There are fewer working people to support the retirees. It has big consequences for taxes, for 55 budgets, for living standards, how people live, and economic growth," notes Mr. Katz. "So it has huge implications, and they really don't know what to do about it."

Projections indicate that by the middle of the 60 century, there will be more than 40, perhaps as many as 50, elderly people per one hundred workers in the United States. In 1940, there were 11 retirees per hundred working-age people. This means that fewer people had to be supported from tax revenues contributed by working people. Many analysts say that unless benefits are cut, taxes to pay for pensions and health care may have to double in the next few decades.

But Ronald Lee, a demographer at the University of California, says that in the United States, where fertility rates are at the replacement level and the work force is regularly replenished by immigrants, the problem is not as acute as in some other industrialized countries. He concedes that the cost of caring for the elderly in the US will increase with the rising health care costs and so some adjustments will have to be made.

"We now live longer and healthier than ever before. Why work shorter? I think the retirement age should be advanced. I think we as individuals, as a culture, and as employers have to be ready to adjust pay scales so that older workers may get declining wages and salaries if their productivity declines," says Professor Lee. "Why take all that leisure at the end of life? I suggest spreading it throughout life and particularly taking more time off during the child-bearing years."

Analysts say aging populations may pose much greater challenges for developing countries where the poverty pressures already strained health care and retirement systems. Despite their rapid economic growth, China and India are still mostly poor societies. China's current government pension system barely covers a fifth of the country's workforce. Its 65-and-older population is likely to double in the next two decades, perhaps reaching as many as 200 million. And, most analysts say, the current pension system will not be able to support it. That means, says Professor Lee, families must start saving for retirement as early as possible.

Demographers predict a host of social and economic changes as the global population ages. Joseph Chamie, Director of Research at the Center for Migration Studies in New York, says many industries will develop new products and services aimed at the elderly.

"Of course, it will also require more people in

Two Chinese women dance at a local community club in the Chinese capital of Beijing. China's rapidly growing elderly population could surge as high as 430 million by 2051, when almost one in three citizens will be 60 or over, posing a grave challenge for already strained state social welfare and pension systems.

(REUTERS/Stringer)

that type of work: health care, nursing, services for the elderly, and so on," says Mr. Chamie. "The entire society will start adjusting to that in terms of its consumption and its products. And you'll see people more concerned about hair color, for example, more and more things about staying young and exercising and staying fit and diet and nutrition and clothing and household things and steps and door knobs and all sorts of things to help people as they get older to continue living productive lives."

Demographers say they are just beginning to understand the broader social, economic, and political implications of the coming "age wave." But, they say, it is clear that governments as well as families and individuals should start preparing as soon as possible.

By Zlatica Hoke Washington, D.C. 30 November 2005
Voice of America

Words and Idioms

Vocabulary
Match each word to its definition.

1. century (*n*) ●	● a. to form part of; to comprise
2. unprecedented (*adj*) ●	● b. to become old; to show the effects or characteristics of increasing age
3. implication (*n*) ●	● c. to become three times as great or as numerous
4. gray (*v*) ●	● d. the quality or state of long life
5. compose (*v*) ●	● e. the quality or state of being able to breed or reproduce
6. age (*v*) ●	● f. a result caused by an action or set of conditions
7. segment (*n*) ●	● g. a period of 100 years
8. triple (*v*) ●	● h. to get gray hair; to turn the color gray
9. fertility (*n*) ●	● i. a fixed sum of money paid to someone who retires from work
10. longevity (*n*) ●	● j. to reduce or lower
11. pose (*v*) ●	● k. having not been done or seen before; new or novel
12. consequence (*n*) ●	● l. the process of getting or giving the right food for good health and growth
13. cut (*v*) ●	● m. to grant or acknowledge
14. pension (*n*) ●	● n. a rounded handle
15. concede (*v*) ●	● o. a separate piece of something; one part of a whole
16. nutrition (*n*) ●	● p. to present; to offer
17. knob (*n*) ●	● q. a result implied; a possible significance

Idioms and Expressions
Fill in the blanks with the correct idiom or expression.

on the rise: increasing in number or size
Obesity is on the rise in the United States.

life expectancy: how long one is expected to live
The average man living in a developed country has a life expectancy of 75 years.

pay scale: measurement of wages
The pay scales between men and women in the same profession can sometimes be unbalanced.

1. Doctors have a higher _____ than street cleaners.

2. Japanese people have the highest _____ in the world.

3. The number of people keeping pets in their homes is _____ in Asia.

Exploring Content

A. Read the statements. Find a sentence in the reading that supports the statement. Write it in the blank.

Example: The number of people worldwide age 65 and over is expected to more than double in the next forty years.

Demographers predict that by mid-century, people age 65 and over will compose about 15 percent of the world's population, up from about seven percent today.

1. The number of people over 65 is going to increase greatly by the year 2100.

   _____

2. Increased life expectancy is a sign of success.

   _____

3. In the U.S., a tax increase might be necessary to help support the aging population.

   _____

4. At present, the system of government in China can only provide for the retirement of a fraction of its total number of workers.

   _____

B. Match the expert with the correct statement.

1. Richard Katz

   a. says population aging is a result of declining fertility rates and increasing longevity

2. William Butz

   b. predicts that industries will develop new products and services for the elderly

3. Ronald Lee

   c. worries about support for retirees

4. Joseph Chamie

   d. favors spreading leisure throughout life

Summary
Fill in the blanks.

life expectancy	aging	triple	cut	consequences
pensions	century	implications	fertility	segment

The world's population is 1 _____ fast, especially in developed countries. The average worldwide 2 _____ has increased from 50 to 65 in the past half- 3 _____. Within the next 100 years, the 4 _____ of the population age 65 and over is expected to 5 _____. This aging population has important 6 _____ for economic growth and well-being of all societies. In the U.S., for instance, it is estimated that unless benefits are 7 _____, taxes may have to double in order to pay for senior citizens' 8 _____ and health care in the coming decades. However, according to Ronald Lee, a demographer at the University of California, the problem in the U.S. is not as acute as it is in other industrialized nations. As 9 _____ rates decrease and longevity increases, countries throughout the world will experience dramatic 10 _____.

Discussion
Discuss these questions with your class.

1. Is the elderly population increasing in your country? How can you tell?

2. What effects, if any, has the over-65 population had on your country's economy? What effects has it had on you personally?

3. How are elderly people treated in your country? Why?

4. In your view, how can countries best support elderly and retired people?

Safety for Kids on the Net

Warm-up

Some people have wonderful stories of how they met their spouse through an Internet chat room. Others, however, have darker tales. The nice person they "met" online was not the same one who showed up face to face. Children are especially vulnerable to such online deception. How can parents and teachers help protect them? How can they teach kids about online dangers?

Points to Notice

Each person mentioned in the article expresses a concern. Pay attention to the words of:

• Casey Walker — a high school technology coordinator
• Jon Bruning — Nebraska's Attorney General
• Jackie Cuttlers — the mother of a 7-year-old
• Jim Teicher — of the CyberSmart Education Company

Cultural Notes and Background

America's individualistic culture, combined with its changing family structure (see Unit 12), allows children plenty of unsupervised time to surf the Net. Nebraska, in the midwestern U.S., has only one major city and a low crime rate, but Internet crime crosses all borders. A recent book, called *Anyone You Want Me to Be*, tells the story of the Internet's first serial killer. John Robinson, a seemingly ordinary father and businessman, used the Internet to lure several young women to his Midwest homes in Kansas and Missouri, where he raped and murdered them. In addition to the precautions described in the article, police are now posing as children and young women in Internet chat rooms in an attempt to prevent crimes against children. They hope Internet predators will invite them to meet in person. Then, they can identify and arrest these criminals.

Nebraska Keeps Kids Safe on the Net

President George W. Bush leans in to talk to Liv Haugen, right, and her sister Solveig, center, in the Roosevelt Room of the White House in Washington, after signing a bill to improve child safety on the Internet. The legislation calls for the creation of a new kids-safe "dotkids" domain on the Internet that would contain only material appropriate for children under the age of 13.

(AP Photo/Pablo Martinez Monsivais)

There is at least one personal computer in two-thirds of America's homes, and more than half of these computers have access to the Internet. Ninety-nine percent of the country's schools have computers, and almost all of them 5 allow students to go online. In other words, it's virtually impossible for a child in the United States to grow up today without using a computer and getting on "the Net." And that's worrying a lot of adults. 10

During a break from classes, Crawford High's technology coordinator, Casey Walker, notes that Nebraska schools have safeguards in place to monitor — and in some cases, control — which websites students visit online. "We're required 15 by law to have a content filter on our Internet here for the K through 12 district," he explains. "There are some filters that are better than others. But it's not foolproof. And the kids have been involved with the computers long enough . . . 20 they know how to type things in here and there that occasionally will get them around. So, you know, it is a good system, but it's definitely not foolproof."

That's why Nebraska has followed the lead of 25 Georgia and Michigan in sponsoring a month-long statewide initiative to promote Internet safety. The state has created a "Safe Kids" website with information on a variety of ways to do that. 30

In addition, Attorney General Jon Bruning toured schools across Nebraska to spread the word about staying safe online. He says April's activities were designed to encourage parents and teachers to take a serious look at what children can access when they go on the Internet and, more importantly, who can find a way to access them.

"We as adults, as law enforcement, can't possibly ensure that all these kids make the right decisions on the Internet," he points out. "But what we can do is give them a little healthy skepticism that when they're on the Internet, people are not always who they seem. And that there is some risk if they carry on a conversation or begin a relationship with somebody on the Internet, there's some risk to them when they do that. And so we're discouraging them, of course, from meeting people on the Internet."

And it's very easy to meet people on the Internet, as Jackie Cuttlers knows. "A lot of the kids get on these sites where they talk back and forth . . . I mean from town to town to all over. The 'chat' things." Her 7-year-old son doesn't go online yet, but she agrees that teachers and parents need to plan ways to be vigilant in monitoring children's use of the Internet. "I've seen a lot of the things that come up and it makes me sick," she says. "I mean . . . for kids, especially the age that they are, I just think there's a lot of things that get 'chatted' about that maybe lead to other things. It worries me."

The National Center for Missing and Exploited Children reports that one in five kids online has been sexually solicited or enticed. Some kids have made friends online and arranged to meet them in person . . . only to discover that they'd been chatting with an adult who wanted something more than conversation. While most teens have heard about 'Internet predators' in chat rooms, many are still willing to share personal information online without considering how it could be misused.

Here at Crawford High, 17-year-old Jill

(Inmagine Corp LLC)

Raben has never encountered the problem herself, but admits "[I] definitely have concerns, because of all what's happened out in the world. I mean, you hear every day [about] girls getting stalked by 40-year-old men and not knowing it. I mean, they're thinking they're the same age." She takes precautions whenever she's online. "I'm not really concerned about me personally because if I'm online and I chat, I know every one of my contacts. I don't go into chat lines, so I'm not as vulnerable to that as some people."

Those vulnerable people include those who use social networking sites like MySpace.com, where anyone can create their own web page, including their name, hobbies and interests, and photograph. Although the minimum age for anyone posting on the site is 16, there is no reliable way to ensure that younger children aren't creating a MySpace page as well. Eighteen-year-old Riley Richardson says that's risky. "People are opening themselves up to such dangers as being stalked or . . . anything. But, it's people's choices."

Unfortunately, some of those "people" are actually young children. According to Jim Teicher, of the CyberSmart Education Company, the best thing parents can do is get online themselves. "Search blog sites, like MySpace, that your child may be visiting . . . may have their own web presence. Do a Google search on your child," he recommends. "Ask, talk to your child, particularly about posting any information on there about themselves, and [make sure] that they do it in a way that someone else could not actually find where they physically are. And the same with a photo. Because once this information is out there, it's gone for good."

In the final analysis, he notes, initiatives like Nebraska's Internet Safety Month can be successful only if teachers and parents carry its message through the other months of the year.

By Jim Kent Crawford, Nebraska 11 May 2006
Voice of America

Vocabulary
Match each word to its definition.

1. virtually (*adv*) ●	● a. to support a movement or event, usually financially
2. safeguard (*n*) ●	● b. a protective device or measure
3. monitor (*v*) ●	● c. to follow or track someone in secrecy
4. filter (*n*) ●	● d. to lure; to attract with some reward
5. foolproof (*adj*) ●	● e. to contribute to the progress or growth of; to further
6. sponsor (*v*) ●	● f. to make sure, certain, or safe
7. promote (*v*) ●	● g. a doubting or questioning attitude
8. encourage (*v*) ●	● h. for all practical purposes; practically
9. skepticism (*n*) ●	● i. perfect; incapable of failing
10. vigilant (*adj*) ●	● j. a person who follows and abuses others
11. solicit (*v*) ●	● k. a measure taken beforehand to prevent harm or to secure safety
12. entice (*v*) ●	● l. to approach with a request or plea
13. stalk (*v*) ●	● m. a tool that separates undesirable material from desirable material
14. precaution (*n*) ●	● n. to increase someone's courage or confidence in doing something
15. ensure (*v*) ●	● o. to display information where the public can see it
16. predator (*n*) ●	● p. the condition of being persistently alert; watchful
17. post (*v*) ●	● q. to watch closely; to keep track of

Idioms and Expressions
Fill in the blanks with the correct idiom or expression.

K through 12: kindergarten through senior high school (12th grade)
Most Americans attend school from K through 12.

follow the lead: to imitate the example of others
I am going to follow your lead and get my Master's degree, too.

spread the word: to tell other people some news or information
The game has been cancelled, so spread the word.

1. In the 20th century, many countries _____ of the U.S. in establishing automobile industries.

2. Our state has the best _____ education in the country.

3. In ancient Greece, messengers ran miles to _____ about the outcome of military battles.

Exploring Content

A. Complete the sentences based on the reading.

1. Casey Walker says Nebraska schools have a good Internet filter system, but
_____

2. Nebraska Attorney General Jon Bruning says schools are discouraging students
_____

3. Jackie Cuttlers says that teachers and parents need to be more vigilant in
_____

4. The National Center for Missing and Exploited Children reports that one in five kids online
_____

5. Jim Teicher advises parents to do a _____

B. Put a check (✔) next to the statements that the writer would agree with.

1. _____ A good filter ensures Internet safety.

2. _____ Most people in online chat rooms are Internet predators.

3. _____ Adults need to help children develop good online judgment.

4. _____ Internet safety months can be useful.

5. _____ Parents in Nebraska don't need to worry about their children using the Internet.

6. _____ It is OK for children to meet chat-room contacts in person.

Summary & Discussion

Summary
Fill in the blanks.

promote	following the lead	predators	vigilant	virtually
safeguards	foolproof	solicited	filters	skepticism

School officials in Nebraska recognize that it is **1** _____ impossible to keep children off the Internet these days. Instead, they are using **2** _____ to help protect students from online dangers such as Internet **3** _____. The law requires schools to have Internet content **4** _____ in grades K through 12. These are good, but not **5** _____. Therefore, the state recently sponsored an Internet Safety Month, **6** _____ of Michigan and Georgia. One of the goals was to help parents learn how to be more **7** _____ in monitoring their children's Internet use. According to The National Center for Missing and Exploited Children, 20 percent of US children have been sexually **8** _____ online. State Attorney General Jon Bruning toured schools across Nebraska to **9** _____ kids' online safety. He said adults can give children a little healthy **10** _____ that when they're on the Internet, people are not always who they seem.

Discussion
Discuss these questions with your class.

1. Have you ever visited an Internet chat room? If so, describe your experience.

2. Have you ever given out any personal information online? How much information do you think it is safe to disclose?

3. How effective are Internet filters? Are there other ways to control children's Internet use?

4. How much do/did your parents monitor your online activity? How does/did this affect your Internet behavior?

Indian Tradition and the Internet

Warm-up

India, generally a culturally conservative nation with many traditions strictly adhered to, is experiencing a strange new phenomenon. The ancient practice of matchmaking — that is, finding suitable marriage partners for single people — is now being conducted via the Internet. This practice is unusual, because the Internet is a very non-traditional example of ultra-modern technology. The motivation behind Internet matchmaking is that it is regarded as more effective and convenient than, for instance, placing advertisements for marriage partners in newspapers. The websites help to simplify the search for partners in this complex, multicultural country where social group and caste are very important. Parents and children of marriageable age are all taking to consulting these sites more frequently.

Points to Notice

As you read, pay attention to the information and opinions associated with each of the following people or concepts:

• Neema Kapur — an Indian fashion consultant
• Vivek Khare — Vice president of Jeevansathi.com, an online marriage brokerage
• Vibhas Mehta — Vice president of shaadi (marriage).com, another Internet broker
• "The main hurdle" to Internet marriage brokering (Paragraph 14)
• The irony of Internet marriage brokering (last paragraph)

Cultural Notes and Background

India is an extremely large country with a very mixed population. People are spread all over this vast sub-continent, speak different languages, dress differently, eat different food, and practice different customs and religions. The two main religious groups are the Hindu and Muslim peoples. It is very unusual for an individual in either group to marry someone with a different belief. Furthermore, the Hindu faith has a caste system. This means one is born into a specific social group and may only marry someone on the same "level" as oneself. The more traditional Indian outlook frowns upon inter-caste marriages. This means that it is even more complicated finding a suitable marriage partner in India than in most other countries, because there are so many rules and restrictions governing one's choice of a husband or wife.

Internet Now Fulfilling Ancient Indian Tradition

A model displays a wedding dress as part of "The Bridal Collection" by Shagun, India's only wedding mall, in Calcutta, India, in 2005.

(AP Photo/Bikas Das)

India, a country famous for arranged marriages, is turning more and more to matrimonial Internet sites to help fulfill this ancient tradition. The web is helping millions of Indians search for the ideal bride or groom. 5

Several months ago, fashion consultant Neema Kapur's 23-year-old daughter asked her mother to find her a marriage partner. It was not an unusual request — in India, parents have found matches for their children since time immemorial. 10

Traditionally, relatives, friends, and marriage brokers have assisted in the hunt for a partner. Later, as communities scattered all over the globe, Indians began placing advertisements in newspapers. 15

But Neema Kapur ignored all these. Instead, she posted her daughter's profile on two matrimonial web sites in hopes of finding a suitable match.

"I can't shut my eyes to this way of finding 20 someone, because this is the best way, I feel," she explained. "Newspapers nowadays seem to be quite outdated, because most of the people are now on the computer."

As many as 1,500 web sites have sprung up in 25 recent years that hold out the promise of locating brides and grooms for young Indians. The larger ones offer services across the country and to overseas Indians, while others restrict themselves to smaller communities. 30

Those surfing the net are not just parents. Many of the users are in the tech-savvy 22 to 35-year age group, who say the web sites are a convenient way to get in touch with people with the specific goal of marriage in mind. They say 35 they are prepared to accept a traditional "arranged marriage," but they would rather locate the right person for themselves.

The technology helps to simplify the search in this complex, multicultural country, where the 40 criteria for choosing partners include not just the usual profession, education, and looks, but also such parameters as language group and caste. The websites have sorted their databases to include all of these. 45

Vivek Khare, the vice president of Jeevansathi.

com, which means "Life Partner," says online marriage brokering is witnessing phenomenal growth because of its simplicity, which newspapers cannot match.

"Space is not a constraint, in a classified [advertisement] you have hardly three or four lines; here you can write much more," he explained. "Secondly, the search is very easy. There you have to browse though all the classifieds; here you can simply do a search based on your criterion. Third, contacting is very simple. You can send an e-mail."

Individual web sites say their membership is growing by leaps and bounds. The largest matrimonial site, Shaadi, or Marriage.com, claims it has seven million members — nearly double what it had two years ago. At least one-quarter of the customers are overseas Indians. Many of the web sites boast that they receive nearly a million hits every month.

It is no surprise, in a country where matchmaking is such an established feature of the culture,

(Inmagine Corp LLC)

that online marriage brokering is becoming one of the most successful Internet businesses.

The matchmaking business is estimated to be worth more than $100 million a year — and matrimonial websites are beginning to capture a chunk of that. A one-month subscription to a matchmaking web site costs between $10 and $20.

As in other countries, subscribing to a web site does not guarantee a partner — although as Neema Kapur relates, India throws some particular obstacles in the way of success.

"I have been able to get two people who have been quite eligible, but for some reason did not work out," she said. "The first one, because the horoscopes did not match, and the second one, the family was too large, and we thought my daughter would not fit into that."

Many of the web sites offer online horoscope services for those who believe in astrology. Some sites are also breaking with conservative matchmaking tradition by setting up sites for divorcees, widowers, and the 40-plus age group.

Companies say the main hurdle to explosive growth is that only about 40 million people in India are estimated to have access to the Internet. Online matrimonial services tend to be restricted for the moment to larger towns and cities.

Vibhas Mehta, vice president of Shaadi.com, says his company is trying to expand its reach to people who cannot log on, by establishing matchmaking centers called "Shaadi points" in various town and cities.

"These Shaadi points are physical centers where a parent or a non-computer-savvy or a non-Internet-savvy person can walk in, talk to the counselors there, put in the profile of their son or daughter, and search for life partners for them from that central data base," he explained. "It is becoming very popular: we already have close to about 90 Shaadi points up and running."

There is irony here. As India rushes towards modernization and entrenched customs begin to change, the information technology for which the country is becoming famous may help carry forward the age-old tradition of arranged marriage.

By Anjana Pasricha New Delhi 15 February 2006
Voice of America

Vocabulary
Match each word to its definition.

1. arranged (*adj*) ●	● a.	having many different cultures
2. tradition (*n*) ●	● b.	one who arranges a suitable match for marriage
3. locate (*v*) ●	● c.	a limit; an obstacle
4. multicultural (*adj*) ●	● d.	the study of the movement of stars and planets and their influence on people and events
5. database (*n*) ●	● e.	to do with marriage and marriage ceremonies
6. phenomenal (*adj*) ●	● f.	organized; prepared in advance
7. constraint (*n*) ●	● g.	suitable; desirable for marriage purposes
8. matrimonial (*adj*) ●	● h.	incredible; great; unusual
9. broker (*v*) ●	● i.	liked or used by many
10. matchmaker (*v*) ●	● j.	to find
11. eligible (*adj*) ●	● k.	something humorous based on opposites or contradiction
12. astrology (*n*) ●	● l.	the process of a society becoming more up to date, or technically advanced
13. savvy (*n*) ●	● m.	a habitual practice of a particular culture
14. popular (*adj*) ●	● n.	to arrange or negotiate a business deal between two parties or groups
15. irony (*n*) ●	● o.	practical knowledge or skill
16. modernization (*n*) ●	● p.	long-established actions or patterns of behavior that have been handed down by previous generations
17. custom (*n*) ●	● q.	an information list stored on a computer hard drive

Idioms and Expressions
Fill in the blanks with the correct idiom or expression.

shut one's eyes to something: to avoid or ignore the truth about something
Terry shut her eyes to her boyfriend's cheating ways.

leaps and bounds: very quickly; to a large degree
Sally's English has improved by leaps and bounds since she started doing her homework more regularly.

break with tradition: to change, adapt, or defy cultural custom
We're breaking with tradition this year and spending Christmas away from home.

1. Estelle _____ when she married a much younger man.

2. People tend to _____ the faults of their loved ones.

3. The new city is growing in _____. The traffic is getting terrible.

Exploring Content

A. Complete the sentences based on the reading text.

1. It was easy for Neema Kapur's daughter to ask her to find a suitable partner because

   _____

2. Online marriage brokering is gaining popularity because newspapers

   _____

3. It is no surprise that matchmaking websites have grown quickly in size and popularity since

   _____

4. By creating sites for divorced people, older singles, or widowed people, these websites are

   _____

5. Online matrimonial services are generally restricted to towns and cities because

   _____

B. Choose the best answer.

1. What is the main idea of the article?
   a. India is a very conservative country, and the Internet is causing social problems.
   b. The Internet is becoming increasingly popular in India as an effective way to provide traditional matchmaking services.
   c. Indian people are using the Internet less frequently to find marriage partners.
   d. India is a country full of lonely single people trying to find love.

2. What can be inferred about Indian society?
   a. Indian society is so liberal that people can marry whomever they want.
   b. Older people in India tend to marry again if they are divorced or widowed.
   c. Indian people like using the Internet.
   d. Indian society is complex due to the many different religions and cultures.

3. Read the following sentence:

   "Companies say the main hurdle to explosive growth is that only about 40 million people in India are estimated to have access to the Internet."

   Which of the following sentences best expresses the essential information in the above sentence?
   a. The biggest problem facing Internet matchmakers is that only a small segment of the Indian population uses the Internet.
   b. The main hurdle for Internet businesses is that 40 million people want to be matchmakers.
   c. The explosive growth of the Indian population is a problem for companies that provide Internet services.
   d. Traditional matchmakers are a hurdle for Internet matchmakers who want to steal 40 million customers from them.

Summary
Fill in the blanks.

eligible	modernization	breaking with tradition	popular	locate
constraints	multicultural	leaps and bounds	custom	matchmaking

Modern Indians are **1** _____ by using Internet **2** _____ web sites in search of **3** _____ marriage partners. The industry has grown by **4** _____, becoming more and more **5** _____. This is chiefly because in this complex, **6** _____ country with so many different religions and languages, one needs special help to **7** _____ a good husband or wife. Newspapers do not offer the same advantages as the Internet, which allows more freedom, a greater selection, and a chance to communicate via e-mail. The Internet has fewer **8** _____ and far more opportunities for people looking for partners. Consequently, the Internet has led to the **9** _____ of an established Indian **10** _____, which may seem rather ironic to some. The fact is, however, that Indians are simply using modern methods to conduct age-old business.

Discussion
Discuss these questions with your class.

1. What do you think of arranged marriages?

2. Do you think one can find a suitable match via the Internet?

3. What are some of the pros and cons of hiring a matchmaker?

4. Do you think it is important to marry someone from the same culture as yourself?

Health Care in India

Warm-up

Ideally, health care is a basic tenet of society. Different countries adopt different approaches to providing health care for their citizens. For India, which has the world's second-largest population, this is a particularly challenging problem. How can a government ensure adequate medical care for more than one billion people?

Points to Notice

As you read, pay attention to some of the particular problems facing Indian health care providers. Keep the following questions in mind as you read.

• What is the primary problem?
• What are secondary problems?
• What solutions have been proposed?

Cultural Notes and Background

India is a bewildering collection of contradictions. In some regions, people live in abysmal conditions, and thousands die from preventable and treatable illnesses. People in other areas, such as the southern state of Kerala, are as healthy as those in developed countries. Only 31 percent of the rural population has access to a potable water supply, and less than one percent enjoy basic sanitation. While life expectancy is rising and infant mortality rates are declining, nearly half the children under age three still suffer from chronic, severe malnutrition. Tuberculosis kills 500,000 Indians each year. Another 100,000 die from respiratory infections, diarrhea, and other illnesses either preventable through clean water, nutritious food, cheap vaccines, or basic drugs.

India Offers Both Best, Worst of Health Care

When Pardip Singh's elder brother fell ill with a severe nerve ailment in a remote village in the eastern state of Bihar, he brought him all the way to New Delhi's All India Institute of Medical Sciences — the country's premier government-run hospital.

Singh had little choice. There were no health centers or doctors near his village who could even diagnose his brother's condition. At the New Delhi hospital, some of the country's best doctors attend to his brother. Twenty-eight-year-old Singh's worries should have ended — but they have just begun.

Singh says he has given up his job as a security guard to stand in long lines with his brother at the hospital. The treatment is free, but to pay for the tests, he has borrowed 350 dollars at a crippling interest of nearly 50 percent a year.

Like Singh, thousands of people flock every day to big public hospitals in Delhi and other cities for treatment.

But in these overcrowded hospitals, they must first battle serpentine lines to see specialists, wait months to undergo tests and surgeries, and spend more than they can afford for board and lodging. Many sick people never gather the resources needed to make the journey and tens of thousands of others borrow money or sell assets to cover expenses.

The head of All India Institute's cardiology department, Srinath Reddy, says one of the primary problems confronting the country is that

An Indian health care worker covers the body of a 5-year-old boy who died of encephalitis at a hospital in Gorakhpur, a town about 265 km (164 miles) east of the northern Indian city of Lucknow. Dozens of children are battling encephalitis here, a disease which is ravaging India's northern states and neighboring Nepal.

(REUTERS/Pawan Kumar)

two-thirds of its billion plus people live in villages — but most hospitals are in big cities.

"We have maldistribution," Reddy explained. "The rural areas and some of the underdeveloped states do not have adequate medical facilities. It is not so much acute lack of vaccines or hospital beds. But most of the beds are in urban areas whereas most of the people are in rural areas, so that is where the problem is."

It is not just advanced care that poses a problem. Even good basic care is inaccessible to the vast majority of people. Thousands of primary medical centers exist, but they are perpetually short of personnel and medicines.

The government, led by the Congress Party, has promised to increase health care services for the rural areas and the poor by appointing community health workers, and implementing a national insurance program — but little has been done so far to meet those goals.

The lack of an effective public health system has led to a booming private system, which takes care of three-quarters of the country's needs.

But the system is unregulated, and poor people are often forced to turn to medical practitioners who are little more than quacks.

Dr. Reddy at the All India Institute is a member of a new private initiative called the Public Health Foundation, which wants to train thousands of public health professionals to meet the country's

Dr. Naveen Bhardwaj helps children afflicted with polio stretch at the Akshay Pratishthan School in New Delhi, India. Of the school's 400 students, about 200 have disabilities. Polio cases have nearly tripled in a six-month comparison over last year in India, one of the world's first polio hubs that was hailed for nearly wiping out the crippling virus. The discovery of new cases is a setback to the world's declared goal of eradicating polio by 2005.

(AP Photo/John McConnico)

vast needs.

"There are no standard guidelines [for] treatment which are universally disseminated and adopted for practice by primary care physicians, there are no quality checks," he said. "And therefore both malpractice which is intentional as well as inadequate medical treatment, these are problems that plague the private sector health care delivery."

The scene is radically different for those who can pay for top-of-the-line private services.

India's million plus doctors include specialists on par with the best in the world.

These doctors staff state-of-the-art facilities that not only cater to middle class Indians but also attract patients from other countries.

That has encouraged a budding medical tourism industry — drawing foreign patients to India for world class treatment at relatively low cost.

New Delhi's Apollo Hospital is at the forefront of this emerging business. Last year it treated 12,000 patients from across the globe — neighboring Bangladesh and Pakistan, to Africa and even developed countries such as the United States, Canada and Britain.

Some people come for knee replacements and heart surgeries for which they may have to wait for months in their home countries, others seek cosmetic procedures that are five to 10 times cheaper in India than in developed countries.

Apollo Hospital's marketing head, Anil Maini, says such hospitals are "centers of excellence." He says once the hospital door is shut, overseas patients never glimpse the urban slums, overcrowding and other problems in India that might erode their confidence in seeking treatment in a developing country.

"Within the four walls of the hospital, we pick him up from the airport and bring him in, he is totally cocooned in the hospital and not exposed to any Third World bane as we say," Maini said.

Fernanda Wagland from Britain was traveling in India with her husband when he was hit by a stomach infection.

She brought him to Apollo Hospital and describes the experience as "pleasant." She may even consider seeking treatment here in the future.

"In England, we would be in the kind of multiple (bed) ward, a bit more hectic, so we are getting more exclusive treatment here. If you really wanted something special done with more care and one-to-one treatment, perhaps one could consider coming here," she said.

The challenge before the country now is to put such high quality services within reach of the poor. Doctors say there is little time to lose — millions in the country suffer from infectious diseases such as tuberculosis and other killers such as AIDS, and lifestyle diseases such as diabetes and heart problems are emerging on a massive scale in rapidly growing cities.

By Anjana Pasricha New Delhi 03 May 2006
Voice of America

Words and Idioms

Vocabulary

Match each word to its definition.

1. premier (adj)
2. diagnose (v)
3. flock (v)
4. serpentine (adj)
5. cardiology (n)
6. acute (adj)
7. perpetually (adv)
8. booming (v)
9. quack (n)
10. disseminate (v)
11. malpractice (n)
12. plague (v)
13. radically (adv)
14. budding (adv)
15. cocoon (v)
16. bane (n)
17. ward (n)

a. severe; demanding urgent attention
b. to be a continual problem; to constantly bother or hinder
c. a person who pretends to be a doctor or who lacks necessary medical skill
d. to gather in a large group
e. to spread; to disperse
f. continually
g. to recognize a disease by signs and symptoms
h. to protect by covering or keeping isolated
i. to a large degree; extremely
j. the study and treatment of the heart
k. long and winding, like a snake's body
l. a source of harm or ruin; a curse
m. at the beginning of a period of growth
n. first in position, rank, or importance
o. a division in a hospital
p. to be growing rapidly
q. a mistake by a doctor that results in injury to a patient

Idioms and Expressions

Fill in the blanks with the correct idiom or expression.

top-of-the-line: the best, and usually the most expensive, of its kind
I bought a top-of-the-line computer last year, but now it is outdated.

on par: equal; on the same level
The author's latest book is not nearly on par with her past works.

state-of-the-art: the newest and most advanced
The new computer uses state-of-the-art graphic technology.

1. The hospital facilities here are _____ with any in the world.

2. These sneakers are very expensive, but they're _____.

3. This TV model was just released last month; it's _____.

Exploring Content

A. Two of the following statements are FALSE according to the passage. Check (✔) the FALSE statements:

1. __ It doesn't cost any money for Indian citizens to go to big public hospitals.

2. __ Private health care handles 75 percent of India's medical needs.

3. __ About 33 percent of India's population lives in villages.

4. __ India's specialists and hospital facilities are among the best in the world.

Rewrite the FALSE statements using information from the passage to make them TRUE.

a) _____

b) _____

B. Choose the best answer.

1. What is the main idea of the article?
   a. India has quality health care, but its system is ineffective in meeting public needs.
   b. India is developing an international reputation for cheap, high-quality medical care.
   c. India's booming private health-care system has effectively met poor citizens' needs.
   d. The Public Health Foundation will train thousands of doctors to meet India's needs.

2. What can be inferred about government-run hospitals?
   a. They lack high-quality doctors.
   b. They aren't really free of charge.
   c. They give top priority to the middle class.
   d. They don't have enough doctors.

3. Read the following sentence:

"New Delhi's Apollo Hospital is at the forefront of this emerging business."

Which of the following sentences best expresses the essential information in the above sentence?
   a. Apollo Hospital is a top-of-the-line budding industry.
   b. Apollo Hospital is a leader in a new business field.
   c. Apollo Hospital obtained new equipment before other hospitals.
   d. Apollo Hospital was the first in New Delhi to employ business managers.

Summary
Fill in the blanks.

serpentine	quacks	booming	top-of-the-line	flock
perpetually	malpractice	on par	state-of-the-art	budding

India has **1** _____ medical facilities, and doctors who are **2** _____ with the best in the world. Still, about two-thirds of its population struggle to get basic health care. People from villages **3** _____ to public city hospitals. Though health care is free, they must wait in long, **4** _____ lines and pay for any necessary tests. There are many primary medical centers providing basic health care, but these are **5** _____ short of medicine and personnel. To help meet health care needs, India has developed a **6** _____ private care industry. However, this system is unregulated, forcing poor people to turn to **7** _____. There are no standard guidelines for primary care physicians, so many poor patients in India experience **8** _____ and a host of other problems. For those who can afford **9** _____ service, the situation is much better. In fact, some facilities are so good that a **10** _____ industry treating foreign patients has now emerged in India.

Discussion
Discuss these questions with your class.

1. Describe a time that you needed to see a doctor or go to a hospital. How much time did it take? How much did it cost? Who paid for it?

2. How does private medical care compare to public medical care in your country?

3. What kind of medical care should governments ensure for all their citizens? What are some ways they could do this?

4. Would you ever consider seeking medical treatment in a foreign country? Why or why not?

Unit 17

Bio-fuels: An Alternative to Gasoline

Warm-up

The world contains only a finite supply of petroleum, the oil refined to make gasoline. As countries become more modernized, the demand for petroleum is increasing rapidly. At the same time, so is the development of alternative energy sources, such as wind, solar, and nuclear power. Now, researchers are exploring the development of other types of gasoline, including fuel derived from beer and corn.

Points to Notice

This passage concentrates on the potential benefits of alternative energy sources, but is vague about the disadvantages. Note the environmental costs of ethanol listed in paragraph 11. What do you think they mean? Can you think of some drawbacks to using biomass, corn stover, and Switchgrass?

Cultural Notes and Background

The United States, with less than a fifth of the world's population, uses almost four-fifths of the planet's energy supply. Numerous studies have shown that conservation — using less energy — can save money and protect natural resources. Yet, in recent years especially, the U.S. government has stressed ways of getting more energy and finding new sources of petroleum rather than simpler measures such as driving less and turning off lights and TVs.

Bio-fuels, a Clean Way Out of Gasoline

Ethanol storage tanks being constructed on the northern port of Santos, Brazil. Ethanol export contracts from Brazil are increasing — a sign that the renewable fuel may be on its way to becoming a world commodity. Brazilian sugar cane mills are getting better deals to sell ethanol fuel abroad by extending what used to be spot market sales into long-term contracts, spurred on by the rise in world oil prices.

(REUTERS/Paulo Whitaker)

The United States, which uses more oil than the next five highest consuming nations combined, not only needs to reduce its demand for petroleum, but also needs to rapidly increase the production of alternative sources of energy. Ethanol, bio-diesel, and the commercial development of what is called biomass (organic matter that can be processed to produce fuels, chemicals, and power) represent the fuels of the future.

Steve Wagner, the Vice President of Merrick & Company in Golden, Colorado, puts his hand into running ethanol. "This is 200-proof ethanol, and it actually would remove the moisture from your skin, it will dry out your skin quite a bit . . . very strong smelling," he said. He is in charge of the ethanol plant built inside the Coors brewing plant, one of the major beer companies in the United States.

Ethanol, made from agricultural and organic products, is abundant, renewable, and clean.

Mr. Wagner describes the partnership between Merrick and Coors. "Coors is not in the fuel business, and Coors was not about to get into the fuel business, so what they did instead was they allowed us to build the unit and actually sell us the brewing residual streams."

For years, brewing companies have paid to dispose of considerably large quantities of organic waste, including yeast condensate, aged discards, spills, and different beers that do not meet their standards. Merrick and Company now uses all of the brewing residuals generated at this plant. But most of the ethanol produced here comes from the yeast drying plant.

Wagner says yeast is a by-product of beer that is utilized in making ethanol. "This is actually dry yeast, for every pound of yeast that you add to the fermentation process when you brew beer, you actually generate about three pounds of additional yeast as they propagate and ferment the beer and the sugars."

Just outside the yeast drying plant are the ethanol tanks. More than 11 million liters of ethanol a year are sent from here to various gas stations in the country.

"What we are doing is taking a waste stream that has a cost associated with disposal and making a revenue stream out of it to the tune of about $6 million a year."

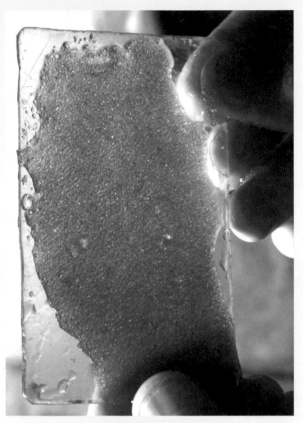

A worker inspects sugar quality in a Sao Francisco mill in Sertaozinho, Brazil. New legislation in Sao Paulo state, Brazil's largest producer of sugar cane, requires farmers to begin phasing out manual methods in favor of mechanized harvesting, to eliminate the need for large-scale burning and its negative environmental impact. Brazil is the world's largest producer and exporter of sugar and ethanol.

(REUTERS/Paulo Whitaker)

Six million dollars is a small amount in the gasoline market. The United States consumes well over 20 million barrels of oil a day. Replacing some of this oil with ethanol seems, so far, to be the most feasible solution to reducing the country's dependence on petroleum.

Today, most cars on the road can use a mix of 10 percent ethanol and 90 percent gasoline. But the car industry is rapidly changing to a higher mix of ethanol.

But relying on ethanol is not without costs. Among the problems is the use of land previously dedicated to the production of food, the impact of a single crop on the soil, and the natural limitations of agriculture.

Susanne Hunt specializes in bio-fuels at the Worldwatch Institute in Washington. "Recent government studies show that we can reach about one-third of our fuel supply with bio-fuels if we used waste residues in this next generation technologies, without causing substantial harm to wildlife, and water, and land resources."

Aware of the limitations of ethanol and bio-diesel, the U.S. government has concentrated its efforts in the research of biomass, derived from crops and agricultural wastes, at the National Renewable Energy Laboratory (NREL) in Denver, Colorado.

"This is corn stover (mature corn stalks of grain with the ears removed that are used as feed for livestock). This is the stock and the husk and the cobs of the corn after the grain has been harvested," says Andy Aden, a process engineer at the laboratory. "One ton of this type of material can typically be made into ethanol to the tune of around 75 gallons of ethanol."

Biomass includes elements such as corn stalks, corn stover, Switchgrass, and a type of wood known as Poplar.

But most of the research is concentrated in the corn stover because of its availability: farmers use some of it on the fields as nutrient and erosion control, but most of it is wasted.

The government is also looking into Switchgrass, a native grass that grows extensively in the plains of the country.

"It could be used as what we call an energy crop where it is specifically grown for energy purposes. It is nice because you can get even more ethanol out of this than what you can get out of an acre (hectare) of corn stover."

At the National Renewable Energy Laboratory, Andy Aden and a team of chemical engineers have proven that the extraction of ethanol from biomass and yeast and sugars works. But their research continues to make the process cost effective. "We're looking into commercializing this probably within the next five to ten years."

But Aden, as many environmentalists, dream of a future of bio-refineries, instead of oil refineries, where biomass can be converted not only into ethanol and bio-diesel but also into biodegradable plastics and chemicals.

By Zulima Palacio Washington, D.C. 12 May 2006
Voice of America

Vocabulary
Match each word to its definition.

1. ethanol (n) ● m ~ _Plant_ ● a. a factory or workshop for the manufacture of a particular product
2. organic (adj) ● g ~ _discant_ ● b. an item or part that is cast off or rejected
3. proof (adj) ● j ~ _Propagate_ ● c. to cause to spread out; to multiply in greater numbers
4. plant (n) ● a ~ _Yeast_ ● d. an organism that promotes alcoholic fermentation, and is used especially in the making of alcoholic liquors and in baking
5. residual (adj) ● h ~ _by-product_ ● e. a material produced in addition to the principal, intended product
6. condensate (n) ● q ~ _stalk_ ● f. the main stem of a plant
7. discard (n) ● b ● g. from or relating to living organisms
8. yeast (n) ● d ~ _residual_ ● h. remaining after the main product is taken out or separated
9. by-product (n) ● e ~ _biodegradable_ ● i. able to be naturally broken down by bacteria or weathering into environmentally safe substances مواد
10. propagate (v) ● c ~ _Proof_ ● j. a standard measure of alcoholic content
11. ferment (v) ● n ~ _ear_ ● k. the fruiting spike of a corn stalk, including both the seeds and protective structures; cob
12. stalk (n) ● f ~ _cob_ ● l. the axis on which the kernels of corn are arranged; an ear of corn
13. ear (n) ● k ~ _ethanol_ ● m. a flammable liquid derived from fermentation
14. husk (n) ● p ~ _Fermend_ ● n. to cause to undergo a chemical reaction in which sugar is converted to CO_2 and alcohol
15. cob (n) ● l ~ _erosion_ ● o. the state of being worn away by water, wind, or ice
16. erosion (n) ● o ~ _husk_ ● p. an outer layer or covering
17. biodegradable (adj) ● i ~ _condensat_ ● q. a material changed into solid or liquid state when a gas is cooled

Idioms and Expressions
Fill in the blanks with the correct idiom or expression.

in charge: in control; in the commanding position
While John is away, Mary will be in charge of the marketing department.

to the tune of: resulting in the approximate amount of
He makes movies to the tune of $4 million per film!

cost effective: able to be sold for more than it costs to make something
It's cost effective to make Coke at 25 cents a bottle and sell it for $1 a bottle.

1. We could make bigger cars, but with high oil prices, they just wouldn't be ___cost effective___.

2. They produce beer ___to the tune of___ four million liters a year.

3. After her father retires, Shelley will be ___in charge___ of the factory.

taozinho, Brazil. New legislation
gest producer of sugar cane, requires farmers to begin phasing
t manual methods in favor of mechanized harvesting, to
minate the need for large-scale burning and its negative
                    Brazil is the world's largest produce

The government is also
                    that grows extensively in the pl

Reading Comprehension Check-up

Exploring Content

A. Two of the following statements are FALSE according to the passage. Check (✔) the FALSE statements:

1. __ Corn stover and Switchgrass are elements of biomass.

2. __ Scientists can extract more ethanol from corn stover than they can from Switchgrass.

3. __ Bio-fuels can be used in about half the U.S. fuel supply without causing substantial environmental harm.

4. __ The main advantage of developing ethanol is to reduce U.S. dependence on petroleum.

Rewrite the FALSE statements using information from the passage to make them TRUE.

a) _____

b) _____

B. Choose the best answer.

1. What is the main idea of the article?
   a. The United States is examining the feasibility of alternative fuels to lessen its dependence on petroleum.
   b. Replacing some oil with ethanol seems to be the most feasible solution to reducing U.S. dependence on petroleum.
   c. U.S. beer companies such as Coors are making money and helping the economy by building ethanol plants and selling their brewing residuals.
   d. Ethanol is abundant, renewable, and clean, but its development also involves environmental costs.

2. What can be inferred about the partnership between Merrick & Co. and Coors?
   a. It is not equally beneficial.
   b. It is outdated.
   c. It is common practice.
   d. It is unique.

3. Read the following sentence.

   "Today, most cars on the road can use a mix of 10 percent ethanol and 90 percent gasoline"

   Which of the following sentences best expresses the essential information in the above sentence?
   a. Most cars today use a mix of 10 percent ethanol and 90 percent gasoline.
   b. Only 90 percent of U.S. fuel consists of gasoline.
   c. Most modern cars are capable of using fuel that is 10 percent ethanol.
   d. Ethanol is replacing gasoline as the primary fuel for U.S. cars.

Summary
Fill in the blanks.

stalks	organic	cost effective	biodegradable	cobs
residuals	ethanol	to the tune of	discards	plant

The United States is trying to decrease its dependence on petroleum and increase its production of **1** _____ and other alternative energy sources. One example of this new trend can be found in the Colorado Coors Beer brewing **2** _____, where Merrick & Co. has been buying Coors' beer **3** _____. Previously considered mere **4** _____, these substances are now being used to make ethanol, thus transforming waste into a revenue stream. Government researchers want to follow a similar model with biomass, which is **5** _____ matter that can be made into fuels, chemicals, and power. One example of biomass is corn stover — mature corn **6** _____ with the ears removed — combined with the husks and **7** _____ of harvested corn. Researchers estimate that one ton of this material can be converted to ethanol **8** _____ 75 gallons. In the future, researchers hope to convert biomass into **9** _____ plastics and chemicals as well. However, the production process is not yet **10** _____. Thus, the research continues.

Discussion
Discuss these questions with your class.

1. Does your country use any other types of fuel besides gasoline? If so, which ones?

2. Which resources could your country use as alternative energy sources?

3. Is it a good idea for a country to reduce its dependence on petroleum? Why or why not?

4. In addition to using alternative fuels, what are some other ways you can think of to reduce petroleum use? Which of these do you consider most feasible?

New Targets to Disrupt HIV

Warm-up

Human Immunodeficiency Virus, or HIV, is the virus that causes Acquired Immune Deficiency Syndrome, better known as AIDS. HIV disables cells in the human immune system that would normally help fight infections and cancers. AIDS is actually a blanket term for various diseases that result from HIV infection. HIV is classified as a "slow" virus, because an infected person may have it for a long time before it develops into AIDS.

Points to Notice

Pay attention to differing comments as you try to determine the significance of the discovery discussed in the passage. Have the researchers found a cure for AIDS? Have they developed a new drug to fight HIV? Note especially the opinions of Dr. Anthony Fauci, head of the US National Institute of Allergy and Infectious Diseases, and the comment about side effects by Stephen Elledge, lead researcher of the new study.

Cultural Notes and Background

About 33.2 million people have HIV or AIDS worldwide, according to the United Nations and the World Health Organization. Almost seventy percent of those people live in Africa. In the United States, it is estimated that more than one million people are living with HIV, and that about a quarter of them do not yet know they are HIV-infected. Since 1981, when the first AIDS case was diagnosed, AIDS has killed more than twenty-five million people, including more than half a million people in the United States.

Researchers Identify New Targets to Disrupt HIV Lifecycle

In what is being hailed as a major step in the fight against HIV/AIDS, US researchers have identified 273 proteins that are key to reproduction of the virus that causes AIDS. As we hear from VOA science correspondent Art Chimes, that gives scientists many potential new targets for drugs to disrupt the sophisticated lifecycle of the virus.

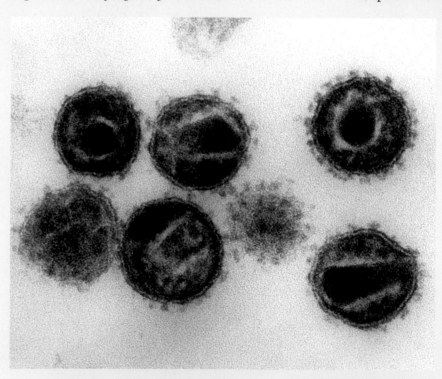

This picture shows an image from an electron microscope, of HIV (human immunodeficiency virus), the virus which is causing the acquired immunodeficiency syndrome AIDS.

(EPA)

Publication of this new study promises to give researchers more avenues to follow as they look for better ways to stop the AIDS epidemic.

"The set of proteins will provide a lot of insight into how the virus actually functions. And people may be able to use that information to somehow circumvent the virus. But the other way you can look at it is that now there are more targets. They're potential targets."

Stephen Elledge of Harvard Medical School, is the lead author of the paper describing the discovery, which was published Thursday online in *SciencExpress*.

HIV has little genetic material of its own, so when it infects a cell, it hijacks the cell's genetic code to reproduce. This new study identifies some of the cell proteins the virus uses in that process.

Speaking in a *Science* magazine podcast, Elledge said current anti-AIDS drugs generally focus on the virus itself.

"But the problem is that HIV is a highly mutable virus, so it can change the target of the drug so that it no longer binds the drug that well."

Which is why Elledge focused on human proteins. Of the 273 he identified as being essential to HIV reproduction, only thirty-six were previously known.

Leading AIDS researchers hailed Elledge's work. HIV co-discoverer, Robert Gallo, called it "terrific." Dr. Anthony Fauci, head of the US 50 National Institute of Allergy and Infectious Diseases, described it as "elegant science," but he told *The New York Times* that it's too soon to tell if this laboratory discovery will actually prove useful in treating patients. 55

Elledge also admits there could be side-effects to any treatments developed using his discovery.

"And the downside, the potential downside, is that if the organism — us — needs that 60 particular protein, [then] if you inhibit it, you might get sick. And of course, that's true for any drug. If anyone finds a drug target and they decide they're going to make a drug that inhibits it, it has to be tested on people to see 65 how people tolerate having that pathway reduced."

To find the 273 proteins that are part of the HIV life cycle, Elledge and his colleagues screened thousands of possibilities using a 70 technique honored with a Nobel Prize a year ago, RNA interference, which can be used to effectively shut down one gene at a time within a cell. Then the researchers infected the cell with HIV to see if the virus could reproduce. 75

"And we did this for over 20,000 human proteins, all the known, currently known proteins to figure out which ones might be important," Elledge explains. "We wanted to cover everything, we wanted to leave no stone 80 unturned to see what the list looked like. And that's how we did it."

Stephen Elledge, of Harvard Medical School

This red ribbon, or AIDS ribbon, is used internationally as a symbol to promote awareness of the deadly disease.

(Shutterstock, Inc.)

and the Howard Hughes Medical Institute, says the same approach could be used to find targets 85 in the fight against other virus infections as well.

By Art Chimes Washington, DC 11 January 2008
Voice of America

Words and Idioms

Vocabulary
Match each word to its definition.

1. protein *(v)* ● b
2. virus *(n)* ● g
3. sophisticated *(v)* ● m
4. epidemic *(n)* ● e
5. circumvent *(n)* ● o
6. genetic *(n)* ● a
7. hijack *(n)* ● k
8. code *(n)* ● d
9. mutable *(n)* ● n
10. bind *(v)* ● i
11. infectious *(n)* ● h
12. inhibit *(v)* ● c
13. infect *(v)* ● f
14. reproduce *(v)* ● j
15. cover *(v)* ● l

● a. relating to genes
● b. a complex, natural bodily substance
● c. to restrain
● d. set of symbols which represent something
● e. something affecting large numbers of people
● f. to contaminate
● g. something that causes disease
● h. capable of infecting
● i. to cause to adhere
● j. to make new life
● k. to commandeer
● l. to go over; to check
● m. complicated; highly developed
● n. changeable
● o. to take an alternative path or method

Idioms and Expressions
Fill in the blanks with the correct idiom or expression.

key: most important
Good health is the key to a long life.

screen: to select or eliminate through preliminary examination
After screening thousands of candidates, four were selected for final interviews.

leave no stone unturned: to exhaust all possibilities
Detectives left no stone unturned in their search for the missing child.

1. Frequent studying is the _____ screen _____ to getting good grades.

2. I use my answering machine to _____ key _____ my calls.

3. The scientists _leave no stone_ in their search for a cure for cancer.

Exploring Content

A. Two of the following statements are FALSE according to the passage. Check (✔) the FALSE statements:

1. __ Researchers know of thirty-six human proteins that are essential to HIV reproduction.
2. __ HIV uses cell proteins to hijack a cell's genetic reproduction code.
3. __ Because it's mutable, HIV can change the target of drugs designed to defeat it.
4. __ Stephen Elledge and his colleagues used RNA interference to screen more than 200,000 human proteins.

Rewrite the FALSE statements using information from the passage to make them TRUE.

a) _____

b) _____

B. Complete the chart based on information from the reading.

Benefits of Elledge's discovery

1. _____

2. _____

Problems with Elledge's discovery

3. _____

4. _____

Summary
Fill in the blanks.

key	circumvent	infects	sophisticated	epidemic
virus	code	reproduce	hijacks	proteins

The recent discovery of 273 human **1** _____ that are **2** _____ to the reproduction of HIV, gives researchers new hope of stopping the AIDS **3** _____. The proteins will provide insight into how HIV actually works, increasing the chances of finding ways to **4** _____ the **5** _____. In its **6** _____ life cycle, HIV uses some of the 273 proteins when it **7** _____ a cell and **8** _____ the cell's genetic **9** _____, which it then uses to **10** _____. Researchers examined more than 20,000 human proteins in order to identify those key to fighting HIV. Though it's uncertain how their discovery might translate into an AIDS cure, it has been heralded as a major step in the battle against the deadly disease.

Discussion
Discuss these questions with your class.

1. How has AIDS affected people in your country? Do you know anyone with AIDS?

2. Scientific research helps us fight the HIV virus once it has infected human cells. What can be done to prevent humans from getting HIV?

3. What other scientific discoveries have you heard of that were important in fighting diseases?

4. What role do you think scientific research will play in the future in relation to human health? Why?

Hero of the Planet

Warm-up

A Chinese proverb says: "Tell me and I forget. Show me and I remember. Involve me and I understand." This is a story of a man who got involved and learned from teachers who have never set foot inside a classroom.

Points to Notice

Read carefully what Mark Plotkin has to say in paragraphs six, eight, and ten. What does this imply about his personal characteristics?

Cultural Notes and Background

The Amazon rainforest in South America is one of the most important and special environments on Earth. Dozens of groups are trying to preserve its ancient trees and plants, which are endangered by the work of farmers and lumberjacks. The rainforest contains hundreds of thousands of species of plants and animals — many of which have not yet been discovered by Western science.

Hero of the Planet

Combines Modern Science and Ancient Tribal Wisdom

Ethnobotanist Mark Plotkin says a night class at Harvard University changed his life. His professor, Richard Schultes, had lived in the Amazon for many years and had written about the medicinal plants of the native peoples. ⁵

Renowned ethnobotanist, environmentalist, and writer Mark Plotkin has been studying healing plants by working with, and learning from, elder shamans of Central and South America for the last 20 years. Plotkin currently serves as President of the Amazon Conservation Team, a not-for-profit organization committed to protecting the biological and cultural diversity of the tropical rainforest.

(www.amazonteam.org)

One evening during a lecture, the professor showed a slide depicting Indians in dark bark-cloth masks and grass skirts. "He said, 'Here you see three Indians of the Yakuna tribe doing the sacred Kai-ya-ree to keep away the forces of ¹⁰ darkness. All of them are totally intoxicated on the hallucinogenic potion made from the yahay vine,'" Plotkin recalls. And when his professor told the class, "The one on the left has a Harvard degree," he was, he says, hooked. "Hooked on ¹⁵ plants, hooked on Indians, hooked on the Amazon."

Plotkin started fieldwork in Suriname, South America, in 1977. His teachers, for the most part, have been shamans, or tribal healers. He ²⁰ says an early mentor named Jaguar Shaman revealed his ferocious, wild animal self to Plotkin in a very scary dream. "I woke up in a cold sweat," he says. "I looked around and there was nothing. It was a dirt floor. There were no ²⁵ footprints."

Jaguar Shaman had been on a hunting trip that night. The next morning Plotkin asked his translator to speak to Jaguar Shaman and communicate the dream. "And, he ran off, and ³⁰ he came back. And I said, 'Did you find him?' He said, 'Yes.' I said, 'Did you give him the message?' He said, 'Yes.' And I said, 'What did he say?' He said that he broke into a big smile and said, 'That was me!'" ³⁵

Plotkin listened and learned. He promised Jaguar Shaman to collect and document the hundreds of plants used by the medicine man. These ranged from painkillers found in the skin of rain forest frogs to antitumor agents based on ⁴⁰ snake venom. The detailed list of natural medicines is the only document in the village — other than the Bible — translated into Jaguar Shaman's native language.

Plotkin, who studied at Harvard, Yale, and ⁴⁵ Tufts Universities, says his fieldwork in tropical America has taught him to open his mind to native ways not easily explained by western science or values. "I think in the world that we live in today (there is) that attitude that we have ⁵⁰ certain technologies, abilities, ideas that can really make the world a better place," he says. "But if we can couple that with some humility and some ability and willingness to learn from others, it is better for us and better for them. So- ⁵⁵ called indigenous people, so-called illiterate people, so-called non-scientific people, have been discovering things long before there was science as we think of it. And, the idea that synthetic chemistry or western medicine or ⁶⁰ western technology has all the answers is equally

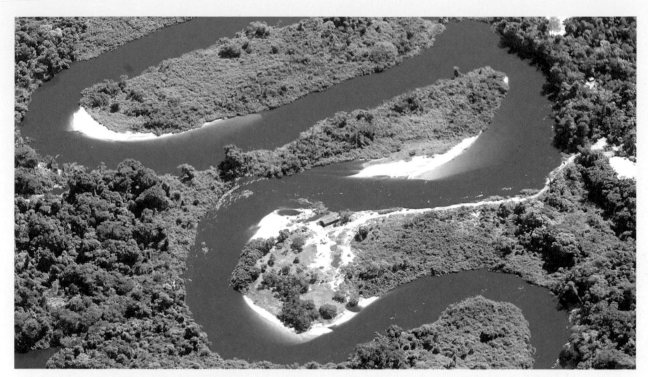

Virgin Amazon jungle is seen in this aerial photo taken over Mato Grosso State, one of the Brazilian states with the greatest deforestation. In the heart of what is known in Brazil as the "arc of deforestation," it is clear that the fight to save the jungle is being lost. During a tour by plane of the area, vast tracts of cleared land with grazing cattle or cultivated fields that have been gouged out of the forest can be seen. The land is irresistible to farmers seeking to expand and benefit from Brazil's agricultural boom.

(REUTERS/Rickey Rogers)

absurd. I think the sweet spot (the truth) is somewhere in between."

Plotkin believes efforts should be made to pass on to future generations the shamans' unique 65 knowledge of the rainforest — knowledge, which he says is often lost when a shaman dies. The Amazon Conservation Team, the non-profit group he directs, runs a Shamans Apprenticeship program that encourages young people to study 70 with elder shamans and learn their ways.

"There are shamans' apprentice clinics set up where traditional healers are practicing traditional medicine," he says. "These are next to clinics set up by missionaries. They have the alternative, 75 the choice, giving more reason to pass on the system of medicine, not just for their benefit, but ideally for the world at large."

The Amazon Conservation Team also supports work to map millions of hectares of ancestral 80 rainforest. The collaboration makes use of NASA satellite photos, handheld Global Positioning System units and shamanic wisdom from those who know the land. Plotkin says, "For example they (the shamans) would say, 'That area is off 85 limits because it is where the two-headed invisible black jaguar lives," Plotkin says. "I don't really personally believe in invisible black jaguars, but it doesn't matter because what they are saying is, it is a headwater area 90 that is off limits to human use and visits and everything else." That makes sense, Plotkin says, because conservationists consider headwaters to be the equivalent of seed corn. "That is the part you have to protect first and 95 foremost."

Ethnobotanist Mark Plotkin has been recognized by the United Nations for his outstanding contributions to the environment. And, *Time Magazine* named him an environmental 100 hero of the planet. "Conservation," Plotkin says, "isn't just about protecting species, plants, and animals. It is about protecting ourselves."

By Rosanne Skirble Washington, D.C. 23 January 2006
Voice of America

Words and Idioms

Vocabulary
Match each word to its definition.

1. ethnobotanist (n) ● m
2. depict (v) ● g
3. tribe (n) ● o
4. sacred (adj) ● k
5. intoxicated (adj) ● j
6. hallucinogenic (adj) ● e
7. fieldwork (n) ● p
8. mentor (n) ● b
9. ferocious (adj) ● f
10. document (v) ● l
11. venom (n) ● a
12. humility (n) ● q
13. illiterate (adj) ● i
14. indigenous (adj) ● c
15. absurd (adj) ● h
16. missionary (n) ● d
17. headwater (n) ● n

- a. a poisonous liquid transmitted by biting or stinging
- b. a trusted counselor or guide; a tutor
- c. originating in a particular region or environment
- d. a person who travels to another place in order to convert others to a religion
- e. able to cause hallucinations, or visions of things not actually present
- f. extremely fierce; savage or cruel; violent
- g. to represent with a picture; to show
- h. ridiculously unreasonable, unsound, or incongruous
- i. unable to read or write
- j. affected as if by alcohol; drunk
- k. worthy of religious veneration; holy
- l. to record; to provide evidence of
- m. a person who studies the practices and beliefs of a group of people as they relate to plants
- n. the source of a stream or river
- o. a social group sharing a common ethnic background and customs
- p. a session of training or research done outside a classroom, on location
- q. the condition of being humble

Idioms and Expressions
Fill in the blanks with the correct idiom or expression.

open one's mind: to cause to consider new ideas or beliefs
The lecture opened her mind to the possibility of life on other planets.

at large: a greater community or area than the one referenced directly; in general
This class is essential not only to English majors, but to university students at large.

off limits: restricted from access or use; forbidden
The street was off limits while the police investigated the murder.

1. Because she failed the quiz, her parents made watching TV _____ for a week.

2. The research conducted here will benefit not only this city, but the world _____.

3. Acupuncture will _____ your _____ to the benefits of alternative medicine.

Exploring Content

A. Complete the sentence based on the reading.

1. Mark Plotkin's teachers have mostly been

_____.

2. Plotkin promised Jaguar Shaman he would collect and document the

_____.

3. Plotkin directs a non-profit group called

_____.

4. Plotkin's group runs a program that encourages young people to

_____.

5. Plotkin's group also helps map

_____.

B. Put a check (✔) next to the statements that Mark Plotkin would agree with.

1. __ Modern science is the most reliable tool for making new discoveries.

2. __ People should keep open minds about things they initially don't understand.

3. __ Conservation is indirectly about protecting ourselves.

4. __ Medicinal plants have little value to the Yakuna tribe.

Summary
Fill in the blanks.

opened his mind	fieldwork	at large	mentor	document
missionaries	venom	humility	ethnobotanist	indigenous

Mark Plotkin is an **1** _____ who became hooked on the **2** _____ culture of Suriname, South America, while studying at Harvard. In the course of his **3** _____, Plotkin helped a Suriname shaman, who was also his **4** _____, collect and **5** _____ hundreds of types of medicinal plants. These ranged from painkillers found in frogs to anti-tumor agents derived from snake **6** _____. In the process, Plotkin learned to combine Western knowledge with **7** _____ and a willingness to learn from others. The shaman **8** _____ to new ideas. Plotkin directs a non-profit group called the Amazon Conservation Team, which sets up shamans' apprentice clinics next to clinics run by **9** _____. This gives apprentices the opportunity to pass on the shamans' medicine to the world **10** _____. Plotkin's team also helps map the Amazon rainforest. Plotkin's work has earned him plaudits from the United Nations and the title "Hero of the Planet" from *Time Magazine*.

Discussion
Discuss these questions with your class.

1. Describe a time that someone opened your mind to something new. What happened?

2. What kinds of plants or herbs are used as traditional medicine in your country?

3. Have you ever tried a type of alternative medicine? Explain.

4. How would you define conservation? Do you agree with Mark Plotkin's definition? Why or why not?

Prescription Sleep Aids

Warm-up

At some point in life, nearly everyone has nights in which they cannot fall asleep. When this problem persists over time, it is called insomnia, and its sufferers may require medical treatment. In America, insomnia is a growing problem. Why do you think this is so? What do you think can be done about it?

Points to Notice

In paragraph three, note the causes of insomnia. Which of these do you think are most relevant? Also, pay attention to the opinion of Dr. Russell Rosenberg. Do you agree with his analysis and treatment recommendations?

Cultural Notes and Background

America is a fast-paced society. The Internet, cell phones, and instant messaging have opened up a new world of instant communication. Some companies require employees to leave their cell phones on at all times. Additionally, Americans continue to work more hours than any other country except Japan. As more and more women have joined the work force, pressure to fulfill everyday responsibilities such as raising children, cooking dinner, and doing housework have increased greatly. At the same time, advertising and marketing techniques are becoming increasingly sophisticated. People are now bombarded with ads even while doing relaxing activities such as eating lunch, surfing the Internet, or watching a movie.

Reading

Popularity of Prescription Sleep Aids Grows

as More Americans Suffer from Insomnia

An estimated 35 percent of Americans experience at least one symptom of insomnia most nights. Emotional stress or excitement can interfere with sleeping patterns, as can some medical conditions, medication, food additives, and caffeine. Poor sleep or lack of sleep is associated with a host of other physical and psychological problems, and more and more sufferers are turning to prescription sleep aids to find relief.

(Yonhap News)

It is something all human beings do, regardless of where they live, how they worship, or what they believe: They sleep. Except that for a growing number of Americans, sleep has become elusive.

Pat Foucht, 67, lives in upstate New York. Eight ⁵

years ago, she developed breast cancer and underwent extensive medical treatments. Ever since, her life has not been the same. "I'm just wide awake all night long," she says. "And sometimes now, I'll wake up and can't get back to sleep. But ¹⁰ it's mainly falling asleep."

Foucht is one of an estimated 60 million Americans who regularly suffer from insomnia, either because they are taking medication, or experiencing pain, or not eating right. Or — ¹⁵ according to Russell Rosenberg, who directs the Sleep Medicine Institute in Atlanta, Georgia — sometimes it is simply because they are living in the modern world.

"It's a 24/7 society now," Dr. Rosenberg notes. ²⁰ "That is, you have Internet 24 [hours], 7 [days a week], television, radio. Everything can keep you distracted from the time you need to sleep. Plus, people are working harder, working more jobs, trying to squeeze in more family-time, more ²⁵ leisure-time and so forth, and so there's only so much time to do the things we want to do in one particular day."

According to an annual poll conducted by the National Sleep Foundation, in 2005, 75 percent ³⁰ of Americans experienced sleeping problems ranging from minor and transient to severe and chronic. That is up from 62 percent in 1999, when the NSF first conducted its poll.

The number of Americans turning to ³⁵ prescription sleep aids for help has gone up even more dramatically: nearly 60 percent over the past five years. American pharmacists filled about 42 million sleeping pill prescriptions last year, and most of them were for either Ambien or ⁴⁰ Lunesta, two recent additions to the sleep aid market.

These drugs are not believed to be habit-forming, and they do not seem to have the same liver-damaging side effects that earlier sleep aids ⁴⁵

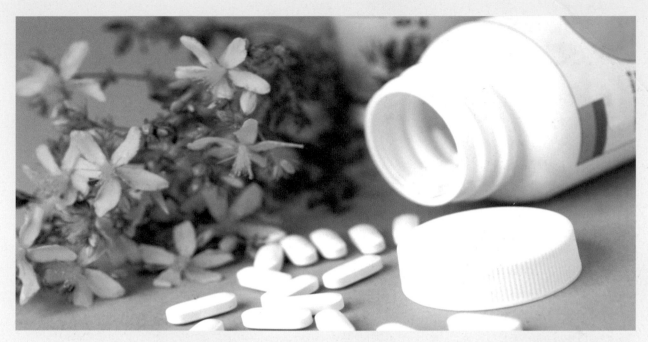

(JupiterImages Corporation)

had. For that reason, Russell Rosenberg says they can be a good option for a particular kind of patient. "For something that we would consider very short-term, or even transient," he says. "Let's say someone had a very serious event in their life, a death of a loved one or something. In the short-run, I think most physicians are going to realize this person just needs a few tablets here and there to get them through the stress of the situation."

At the same time, there is some evidence that these new sleeping pills may not be completely harmless. Some people who have taken them have reported having short-term amnesia. And Pat Foucht says she definitely feels side effects the morning after she has taken a prescription sleep medication. "I do take something now when I have this problem, and I've found that I'm groggy in the morning when I take it. And also I may be a little bit more depressed."

For that reason, sleep experts prefer to treat their patients with what is known as "cognitive behavioral therapy," or CBT. It is a form of psychotherapy that tries to change the way a patient thinks, feels, and acts about sleep.

It does not yield immediate results, though, and in many parts of the country, it is unavailable. There are only about 200 clinicians worldwide who have extensive CBT training in the area of sleep. That is part of the reason prescription drugs have become so popular.

But the biggest reason, says Gregg Jacobs, an assistant professor of psychiatry at Harvard Medical School, is marketing. "You'll see their ads every night on television now. They're the most frequent drug ads on TV," he notes. "As a result, people around the United States — and soon around the world — are being given the message that you can take a sleeping pill, and it will cure your insomnia. And when people hear that, they rush out to buy this pill."

Last year, drug companies spent more than $300 million on ads for prescription sleep aids. That is more than four times as much as they spent in 2004.

But Gregg Jacobs has unveiled his own weapon in the battle against insomnia. It is an interactive website, cbtforinsomnia.com. Patients sign on and have regular telephone and Internet consultations with a trained clinician who could be two or 2,000 kilometers away. Results from a study funded by the National Institutes of Health indicate that Internet based CBT may be more effective than prescription medication or even face-to-face therapy when it comes to treating insomnia.

By Maura Jane Farrelly New York 24 February 2006
Voice of America

Vocabulary
Match each word to its definition.

1. prescription *(n)* ● 1

2. insomnia *(n)* ● e

3. upstate *(adj)* ● j

4. extensive *(adj)* ● o

5. conduct *(v)* ● f

6. transient *(adj)* ● c

7. chronic *(adj)* ● b

8. pharmacist *(n)* ● a

9. tablet *(n)* ● p

10. amnesia *(n)* ● d

11. groggy *(adj)* ● i

12. depressed *(adj)* ● n

13. cognitive *(adj)* ● k

14. psychotherapy *(n)* ● q

15. yield *(v)* ● g

16. psychiatry *(n)* ● h

17. unveil *(v)* ● m

● a. a person licensed to prepare and dispense drugs

● b. marked by a lengthy or permanent duration

● c. brief in duration or stay

● d. a loss of memory

● e. the inability to get enough sleep

● f. to direct and control; to do

● g. to produce; to result in profit

● h. the study and treatment of mental conditions

● i. not fully awake or mentally alert

● j. related to northern sections of New York state

● k. related to the act or process of thinking or knowing

● l. a doctor's written direction for medicine

● m. to reveal; to introduce

● n. feeling very unhappy

● o. covering a broad range or area

● p. a pill

● q. the treatment of a mental or emotional disorder through psychological means

Idioms and Expressions
Fill in the blanks with the correct idiom or expression.

24/7: all the time; 24 hours a day, seven days a week
The doctor's partner was out of town, so she was on call 24/7 last week.

side effects: unintended consequences, usually associated with taking medicine
Aspirin often produces negative side effects on the stomach.

rush out: to act quickly
Shoppers rushed out to buy the DVD as soon as it was released.

1. People are ___Rushing out___ to watch that new movie.

2. Most hotels are open ___24 /7___.

3. The ___side effects___ of this cold medicine include drowsiness and nausea.

Exploring Content

A. Complete the sentences based on the reading text.

1. According to Russell Rosenberg, people sometimes suffer from insomnia just because
   they are living in the modern world

2. The number of Americans getting prescription sleep aids has gone up
   nearly 60 percent over the past five years

3. CBT tries to change the way a patient
   thinks feels add acts about sleep

4. CBT does not _yield immediate results_, and in many parts of the US
   it is un available

5. Last year, drug companies spent _more than $300 million_ on ads
   for prescription sleep aids.

B. Find a synonym in the reading.

1. Find a word in paragraph 3 that means **manages**.

   _____

2. Find a verb phrase in paragraph 4 that means to **make room for**.

   _____

3. Find a term in paragraph 8 that means **temporary**.

   _____

4. Find a word in paragraph 11 that means to **heal** or **fix**.

   _____

5. Find a verb phrase in paragraph 13 that means to **enter an Internet site**.

   _____

Summary
Fill in the blanks.

conducted	psychotherapy	insomnia	chronic	yielded
rushing out	amnesia	side effects	unveiled	prescriptions

A good night's sleep has become elusive for millions of Americans who suffer from
1 _____. According to a poll **2** _____ by the National Sleep Foundation,
about 75 percent of Americans experienced sleeping problems ranging from minor to
3 _____ in the year 2005. To help deal with this problem, Americans are
4 _____ to buy sleep aids. American pharmacists filled **5** _____ for 42
million sleep aids in 2005. Though two new kinds of sleeping pills claim to have no
6 _____, some people who have taken them have suffered short-term
7 _____. A few doctors are now trying to treat insomnia with **8** _____,
but this treatment has not **9** _____ immediate results. One researcher, however,
has recently **10** _____ a promising solution — Internet-based psychotherapy.
Initial studies show that this might be the most effective way to fight insomnia.

Discussion
Discuss these questions with your class.

1. Have you ever suffered from insomnia? What are some ways you tried to get to sleep?

2. Have you ever suffered side effects from medication? Describe your experience.

3. How are drugs such as sleep aids marketed in your country? Through which types of media are drugs advertised?

4. What do you know about psychotherapy? Do you think it is, or could be, an effective treatment? Why or why not?

Unit 21

Writers Demand Human Rights

Warm-up

"Human rights" is a broad term that refers to certain freedoms deemed essential for all individuals, no matter where they live. Today, as throughout history, different countries have different opinions about what basic human rights should be. Many people have protested, and even died, in an effort to gain what they consider to be human rights for people all over the world.

Points to Notice

As you read, think about what PEN, the worldwide association of writers, is actually trying to do. Pay attention to the statements of these individuals:

• Larry Siems — the head of PEN's international program

• Salman Rushdie — a controversial author

• Li Jianhong — a Chinese human rights lawyer

What is PEN asking for? How does it propose to accomplish its goal?

Cultural Notes and Background

In the United States, as well as in Britain and other Western countries, freedom of expression is considered a cherished right. The US Constitution, with a few limitations, allows all citizens to freely express their thoughts and opinions in speech and writing. If something is true, it is permitted to be printed or broadcast, even if the truth embarrasses or hurts someone. This concept applies especially to public figures — such as government leaders, and sports and movie stars — who experience less protection from harmful publicity than ordinary, private citizens. Also, if citizens disagree with something their government is doing, they routinely express their opinions with letters, phone calls, protests and petitions. If enough people express their views, they can cause government leaders to change their policies.

Writers Demand China Release Imprisoned Writers

Three thousand members and supporters of PEN, the international writers' group, have signed a petition demanding the release of imprisoned writers in China. From VOA's New York Bureau, correspondent Barbara Schoetzau, reports that the group presented the petition to officials at China's UN mission in New York ninety-nine days before the opening of the Beijing Olympics. ⁵

Members of the PEN American Center say ¹⁰ the petition is simply asking the Chinese government to live up to the pledge Beijing made to improve its human rights record when the nation secured the Olympic Games in 2001. ¹⁵

Larry Siems, the head of PEN's international program, says the group is not calling for a boycott of the Olympics, but is pressuring

Writers deliver a petition at the Chinese Mission to the United Nations on Thursday May 1, 2008 in New York. The petition demands the release of thirty-nine writers and journalists imprisoned in China believed to have been jailed for exercising free speech.

(AP Photo/Jason DeCrow)

Author Salman Rushdie photographed on May 13, 2008. Rushdie is one of the most well-known victims of attempted threats and censorship due to his writing on controversial topics.

(*The New York Times*/Nicole Bengiveno)

governments to make sure Beijing complies with its promises.

"We are addressing ourselves not only to the Chinese government but to our own governments," said Larry Siems. "PEN is an international organization. In every country of the world where there is a PEN Center, PEN members are asking their own governments to make this a top priority in all of their discussions with the Chinese authorities during the Olympic year."

PEN believes thirty-nine writers are currently being held in Chinese prisons. Human rights lawyer Li Jianhong represents five of them. On Monday evening he accepted PEN's *Freedom to Write* award on behalf of one of his imprisoned clients, Internet writer Yang Tongyan, who is serving a twelve-year sentence for writing articles critical of the Chinese Communist Government. Li, who has lost his license to practice law, says human rights cannot exist in a country where people can be arrested for simply speaking or writing.

"We all know that freedom to write is the right for all writers," said Li Jianhong. "But for a Chinese writer it is simply a dream. For Chinese writers, freedom in politics is not the priority, the freedom to write is our priority."

Author Salman Rushdie is one of the literary world's best-known victims of attempted censorship and threats. He spent almost a decade living underground after one of his novels provoked violence in some Muslim nations and a fatwa, calling for his death. Rushdie says pressure from PEN can be effective.

"Totalitarian regimes are oddly susceptible to being shamed in public," said Salman Rushdie. "They don't like it. They have this odd desire to be popular. So, if you can say loudly enough the things that make them ashamed, PEN has a long history of getting writers out of jail in very oppressive regimes because the government was ashamed of the spotlight. So it is very important to make the spotlight as bright as we can."

The petition also calls on Beijing to stop detaining, harassing, and censoring writers and journalists in China, to end Internet censorship, and to reform laws that suppress freedom of expression.

By Barbara Schoetzau New York 01 May 2008

Vocabulary
Match each word to its definition.

1. petition *(n)*	●	● a.	agreement; promise
2. pledge *(n)*	●	● b.	punishment after conviction
3. secure *(v)*	●	● c.	unable to guard against or vulnerable to
4. boycott *(n)*	●	● d.	to cause
5. pressure *(v)*	●	● e.	written request
6. address *(v)*	●	● f.	oppressive government
7. sentence *(n)*	●	● g.	confront; analyze; look at
8. provoke *(v)*	●	● h.	severely burdensome
9. fatwa *(n)*	●	● i.	refusal to participate
10. regime *(n)*	●	● j.	to forcibly hold
11. susceptible *(adj)*	●	● k.	to cause humiliation
12. shame *(v)*	●	● l.	to suppress; delete
13. oppressive *(adj)*	●	● m.	to influence action
14. detain *(v)*	●	● n.	Islamic decree
15. censor *(v)*	●	● o.	to ensure possession of

Idioms and Expressions
Fill in the blanks with the correct idiom or expression.

live up to: to honor or fulfill
The soccer player never lived up to his potential.

top priority: most important
Make this task your top priority.

spotlight: publicity
She gets nervous in the spotlight.

1. Ending the war was a _____ for the president.

2. A famous artist once said that everybody gets fifteen minutes in the _____.

3. If you make a promise, you should _____ it.

Exploring Content

A. Read the statements. Find a clause or sentence in the reading that supports the statement. Write it in the blank.

1. PEN does not want to disrupt the Beijing Olympic Games.

_____.

2. Li Jianhong believes freedom to write is very important.

_____.

3. Salman Rushdie has been in trouble for his writing.

_____.

4. PEN has been effective in the past.

_____.

B. Put a check (✔) next to the statements that Larry Siems would agree with.

1. __ Writers should be treated differently in different countries.

2. __ The US government should demand that China improves its human rights.

3. __ Countries should refuse to participate in the Olympics until China frees its jailed writers.

4. __ Publicly shaming governments is an effective strategy for change.

Summary
Fill in the blanks.

live up to	censoring	shame	pressuring	detained
spotlight	top priority	petition	boycott	regime

PEN, the international writers' group, wants the Chinese government to **1** _____ its vow to improve its human rights record on the eve of the Beijing Olympic Games. About 3,000 PEN supporters have signed a **2** _____ demanding that China release an estimated thirty-nine writers currently being **3** _____ in prison for writing deemed critical of the Socialist **4** _____. In addition, PEN wants China to stop harassing and **5** _____ writers. Though PEN does not advocate an Olympics **6** _____, it does want to **7** _____ Beijing by putting it in the worldwide **8** _____. PEN is doing so by **9** _____ national governments around the world to make this issue a **10** _____ during discussions with their Chinese counterparts.

Discussion
Discuss these questions with your class.

1. How much freedom do writers in your country have? Are there certain topics they are not permitted to write about?

2. Do you agree with PEN that the freedom to write should be a top human rights priority? Why or why not?

3. What do you think of the strategy of shaming governments? Is it effective? Why or why not?

4. What are some other methods groups or individuals can use to provoke changes? Which would work best in your country?

Women: Their Unique Beauty

Warm-up

What is beauty? Different cultures define it differently. For example, large women have been considered beautiful for centuries in many parts of Africa. In the United States, however, thin women have been the standard of beauty for the past several decades. In recent years, with the advent of the Internet and satellite TV, this U.S. concept of what's beautiful has spread to cultures all over the world. Pressured by the advertising and entertainment industries, women are resorting to all kinds of methods, including plastic surgery and dieting, to conform to this notion and to make themselves appear more "beautiful" — at least on the outside.

Points to Notice

Besides Eve Ensler, consider what others who are quoted in the article have to say. Compare Ensler's ideas with comments by the following individuals:

• Dominique Dawes — a gold-medal gymnast
• Nancy Etcoff — an author and self-esteem expert

Do these women agree on the cause of young girls' low self-esteem? Do they agree on the solution?

Cultural Notes and Background

Dieting and beauty aids are multimillion-dollar businesses in the U.S. It is estimated that Americans spend an average of $109 million each day on dieting and diet-related products alone. In America and the U.K., an estimated 15 percent of young women suffer from eating disorders, which cause them to become unhealthily thin. Also, plastic surgery and non-surgical cosmetic procedures in the United States rose by almost 200 percent between 1997 and 2004. The Asia-Pacific region is not far behind. China, for example, now has more than 10,000 institutes that perform cosmetic surgery, and the industry there is expected to double its 2003 revenues of 2 billion RMB ($240 million U.S.) over the next three years.

This undated publicity pho... Isabella Rossellini in Ensler's one-wo... York's Booth Theatre. (AP Photo/Joa...

Playwright Eve Ensler, Others Encourage Women

to Embrace Their Unique Beauty

Faced with the unattainable beauty standards promoted by the entertainment and advertising industries, many women have become unhappy with the way they look. They are constantly dieting and trying to alter one part of their body or another. But there is a growing movement to encourage women to accept their bodies as they ⁵ *are and to look beyond the commercial definitions of beauty.*

This undated publicity photo shows Eve Ensler performing as Isabella Rossellini in Ensler's one-woman show, *The Good Body*, at New York's Booth Theatre.

(AP Photo/Joan Marcus)

In her new one-woman play, *The Good Body*, ¹⁰ Eve Ensler portrays female characters of different shapes, colors, and cultural backgrounds. Each is based on a real woman the feminist playwright met and talked to as she traveled the world. She says wherever she goes, she finds there is an ¹⁵ image of beauty that women feel compelled to conform to.

"For example, you can go to tribes in Africa where they have fattening rituals for brides," she says. "And you come to Los Angeles and you have ²⁰ to be a certain kind of skinny. Then you go to Iran where women are having nose jobs so their noses don't look Iranian. I spent a lot of time in Istanbul, where women are obsessed with getting rid of their [body] hair. They do tons of ²⁵ sugar waxing. They spend their lives just ripping off their hair."

Ensler says the global reach of Western media — movies, television, and magazines — is changing the concept of 'what's beautiful.' "For ³⁰ example, in India, younger women now are obsessed with being skinny," she says. "It's beginning to happen everywhere in the world. Eating disorders are on the rise in China. They did this poll in Bali where after [the American TV ³⁵ show] '90210' had been on TV for a few months, eating disorders tripled."

In the United States, girls as young as 12 or 13 are trying to remake themselves, according to Nancy Etcoff, author of *Survival of the Prettiest*. ⁴⁰ "By the seventh grade, half the girls are already saying that they don't like the way they look," she says. "The majority, now, are dieting, using food substitutes in order to lose weight. We see young girls going to extreme measures, using laxatives, ⁴⁵ or vomiting, or using dieting pills."

Women's Sports Foundation president-elect and three-time Olympic gymnastics medalist Dominique Dawes, left, and Olympic gold medalist Kristi Yamaguchi arrive at the Women's Sports Foundation's Salute to Women In Sports awards dinner in New York, Oct. 18, 2004. Each year the foundation honors the best athletes in women's sports, including the Sportswoman of the Year.

(AP Photo/WSF, Jim Sulley)

Gold medal gymnast Dominique Dawes says most of those girls do not need to lose weight at all. "I found through research that between 50 and 70 percent of young girls who describe ⁵⁰ themselves as overweight are actually of normal weight," she says.

However, many girls feel pressured to look a certain way. "That's a problem, when a young girl is looking in the mirror, she's seeing a distorted ⁵⁵ image," Dawes says. "That's because of this narrow definition of beauty that's portrayed daily, constantly, on television. She is not seeing the beauty and the strength that we may see."

The former Olympian is now spokesperson ⁶⁰ for Uniquely Me, a program co-sponsored by the Girl Scouts of America to boost girls' self-esteem and help them feel good about themselves. "I've spoken to many young girls and it's very obvious when a girl has a self-esteem problem," she says. ⁶⁵ "She doesn't want to challenge herself. She's okay with being the spectator because she's afraid of what people may say or think about her if she does not live up to winning or certain standards of achievement." ⁷⁰

Self-esteem expert Nancy Etcoff says parents, especially mothers, can help their daughters find their real beauty. "One is to be a role model," she says. "Mothers have to show their girls that they have confidence in themselves, that they see the ⁷⁵ beauty in their daughter, that they are not following the stereotypes of beauty themselves. So women have to really do some self-examination here. How have these media influences impacted them? What support would they have liked as a ⁸⁰ young girl from their mother?"

Playwright Eve Ensler agrees. She says every woman has the right to develop her own concept of beauty, and it all starts in the family. "If you live with a mother who hates her body, you will ⁸⁵ absolutely hate your body," she says. "If you live with a mother who says to you every minute, 'If you're skinny, everything will work out with you,' you'll be skinny and obsessed with being skinny. It only takes two sentences. You only need to say ⁹⁰ it twice or maybe even once and girls get it. So part of it is how mothers and fathers pass on a different idea of beauty, a different idea of what women are worth, and how women are evaluated, not based on their skinniness or fullness, but ⁹⁵ based on their intelligence, their heart, their spirit, their ability to take risks and be bold."

If women don't respect their bodies and accept themselves the way they are, Ensler says, they're wasting their resources and missing out on more ¹⁰⁰ important goals in life. Instead of fixing their bodies, she suggests, women should start to work on fixing their communities and the whole world.

By Faiza Elmasry Washington, D.C. 23 February 2006

Vocabulary
Match each word to its definition.

1. unattainable *(adj)* ●   ● a. a person who believes that men and women should have equal rights

2. alter *(v)* ●   ● b. to urge; to drive forcefully or irresistibly

3. distorted *(adj)* ●   ● c. a drug taken to loosen the bowels and relieve constipation

4. commercial *(adj)* ●   ● d. to play the role of; to depict

5. portray *(v)* ●   ● e. not able to be obtained or secured

6. feminist *(n)* ●   ● f. the level of confidence and sense of worth a person feels for him- or herself

7. playwright *(n)* ●   ● g. an idea; a way of thinking

8. compel *(v)* ●   ● h. twisted out of a natural, normal, or original condition

9. concept *(n)* ●   ● i. a standardized idea that represents an oversimplified opinion, prejudiced attitude, or superficial judgment

10. obsess *(v)* ●   ● j. a person chosen to speak officially for a group

11. laxative *(n)* ●   ● k. viewed with regard to profit; designed for a large market

12. spokesperson *(n)* ●   ● l. to affect; to influence

13. boost *(v)* ●   ● m. to change slightly

14. self-esteem *(n)* ●   ● n. a person who watches something

15. spectator *(n)* ●   ● o. a person who writes plays

16. stereotype *(n)* ●   ● p. to increase; to bolster

17. impact *(v)* ●   ● q. to think about too often

Idioms and Expressions
Fill in the blanks with the correct idiom or expression.

nose job: plastic surgery to alter the nose
My nose looks shorter; I had a nose job last month.

go to extreme measures: to take disproportionate or desperate action
I'm going to take extreme measures to earn money; I'm going to work three jobs.

role model: an example for others to imitate, especially children
John's mother doesn't think rap singers make good role models.

1. He _____ to find tickets to the World Cup final.

2. Sarah's _____ makes her look 10 years younger.

3. Many people in their teens try to emulate _____ they see on TV.

Exploring Content
A. Complete the sentence based on the reading.

1. Eve Ensler says that wherever she goes, she finds there is an image of beauty that women
_____.

2. According to Ensler, the global reach of Western media
_____.

3. Nancy Etcoff claims that half of U.S. seventh-grade girls
_____.

4. Dominique Dawes says research shows _____
_____ of young girls who think they are overweight really aren't.

5. Etcoff and Ensler agree that the concept of beauty
_____.

B. Put a check (✔) next to the statements that Eve Ensler would agree with.

1. __ Mothers are the most important role models for developing girls' concepts of beauty.

2. __ It is good for women to get nose jobs if it improves their self-esteem.

3. __ Women should have a higher social status than men.

4. __ It is important for women to contribute to their community and help others.

Summary
Fill in the blanks.

obsessed	self-esteem	concepts	unattainable	alter
portrays	commercial	extreme measures	role models	compelling

Women worldwide, influenced by **1** _unattainable_ definitions of beauty, have become unhappy with the way they look and are trying to **2** _alter_ their appearance. Playwright Eve Ensler explores this topic with a new one-woman play, called *The Good Body*, in which she **3** _____ real women she has met. She says the Western media has influenced **4** _concepts_ of beauty throughout the globe, **5** _compelling_ women to feel the need to remake themselves through dieting, surgery, and other **6** _extreme measures_. However, gymnast Dominique Dawes says most girls don't need to lose weight. Instead, they need to boost their **7** _self-steem_. In this respect, parents must serve as **8** _role models_ in developing their children's concepts of beauty. If mothers are **9** _____ with being skinny, their daughters will be, too. Instead, Ensler urges parents to emphasize the unique beauty each child possesses and stop trying for **10** _____ standards.

Discussion
Discuss these questions with your class.

1. What types of women are considered beautiful in your culture?

2. How does the media in your country influence concepts of beauty?

3. What are the top five qualities you would look for in a potential spouse? Where does physical beauty rank on your list?

4. In which ways have your parents influenced your concept of beauty? In which ways have other role models influenced your concept of beauty?

Unit 23

Martin Scorsese: America's "Real" Director

Warm-up

Some people watch movies to escape everyday life. Others enjoy seeing "real life" reflected on the screen. Director Martin Scorsese falls into the latter category. His works include three movies named among the American Film Institute's 100 best of all time: *Taxi Driver, Raging Bull*, and *Goodfellas*.

Points to Notice

Think about the impact Martin Scorsese's childhood had on his film career. What does he say about his experiences growing up? Note also the comments of actors Leonardo DiCaprio and Matt Damon. What is the recurring theme throughout the passage? If you had to sum up Scorsese's movies in one word, what would it be?

Cultural Notes and Background

Americans have always loved to watch movies. About 1.4 billion US citizens purchase cinema tickets to attend about 600 new movies each year, according to the Motion Picture Association of America. Though films are now made in many different locations, Hollywood — in Southern California – remains synonymous with movie-making all over the world. As with movies, violence and organized crime have always been staples of American culture. The Mafia, the most famous group of organized criminals, has inspired some of the best and most famous American films, including *The Godfather* trilogy and Scorsese's *Goodfellas*.

Martin Scorsese Provides Unblinking Look at America's Mean Streets

Martin Scorsese's gritty and realistic films consistently earn top critical praise and helped define American cinema over the past four decades. Alan Silverman has more on the director who was just honored by the Kennedy 5 *Center for the Arts as "a true original; a fearless artist who brings out the best and most inspired work in others and in the process continues to surpass himself."*

In this promotional photo released by Miramax, Martin Scorsese, left, directs actor Leonardo DiCaprio in the film *The Aviator*.

(AP Photo/Miramax)

They are some of the most honored films of 10 this generation: *Taxi Driver* and *Mean Streets* in the 1970's; in the 80's, what many still consider the best movie about boxing ever, *Raging Bull*; the 1990's brought the ultimate mobster drama, *Goodfellas* as well as a story of 15

Tibetan spiritualism in *Kundun;* and he continues in the new century with *The Aviator* and *The Departed*.

The man who created those lasting film images and many more, Martin Scorsese, was 20 born in New York in 1942. Severe asthma kept him from sports or other activities, so he spent much of his youth in the inviting darkness of a neighborhood cinema. "I will never forget watching William A. 25 Wellman's *The Public Enemy* with Jimmy Cagney when I was ten years old . . . in a theater on a re-release," he says. "The brutal honesty of that film, the 30 'street' honesty of it, always stayed with me and that's a mark I always aim toward."

Perhaps it is not surprising that a 1931 gangster film made 35 such an impression on the young Scorsese. It is a milieu that the Italian-American director has revisited often in his own films and that he says 40 he knew first-hand growing up in the New York of the 1940's and '50's. "It isn't that I met them," he explains, "it was more living in a working 45 class environment. Part of that environment was organized crime, there is no doubt about that, but it's a difficult thing to talk about because the people who were trying to live a daily life and provide for their families always 50 get offended by this sort of thing." He says,

Director Martin Scorsese holds up his Oscar for Best Director in *The Departed* at the 79th Annual Academy Awards held at the Kodak Theater in Hollywood, California, on Sunday February 25, 2007.

(EPA/Paul Buck)

with a wry smile, his old friends always complain to him about the pictures that he makes.

As a teenager from a very devout Roman Catholic family, Scorsese entered a seminary to study for the priesthood; but film turned out to be his true calling and he switched to New York University where he studied the craft and even taught for a while. Among his students was a young Oliver Stone.

From the beginnings of his filmmaking career in the 1970's, actors learned to respect his passion for storytelling with characters audiences can believe are real. Leonardo DiCaprio, who starred in *The Aviator and The Departed*, says "What I love about Mr. Scorsese's work is that he not only gives the same appreciation to the entire film and the construct of the film, but he really lets the audience engage with every character, no matter how small they are. Each character is fulfilling."

His *Departed* co-star, Matt Damon, says that the world of a Scorsese film, while not necessarily a comfortable place to be, always seems real. "In all of his films there is an authenticity that you just can't fake. It's because he uses a lot of real people and because his actors have access to these real people to get as much understanding of the people they are playing," he explains. "Ultimately it's a giant magic trick. We're just trying to be believable."

The world of a Scorsese film is often shattered by violence. The director says that comes from a reality he observed while growing up. "The violence in my own films . . . I can't defend it, but I approach it the way I experienced it and I know what I saw. I was very affected by it, and I can tell you, more than the physical violence it was the emotional violence around me. It's part of what I am and who I am . . . and somehow it channels itself into the films. I see it sometimes as absurd, but that's just the absurdity of being alive."

What many consider absurd, especially those who worked with him, is that despite all the praise for and influence of his films, Scorsese had not been given Hollywood's top honor, the Oscar. That changed in 2007 when he took home the gold statuette as Best Director for *The Departed*.

"It's a good thing I didn't get it before," he admits, "because maybe it would have changed the kind of movies I made or something. I couldn't trust myself. I don't know if I was strong enough to have gotten it before, quite honestly. The incredible thing is I got to make these movies that I really wanted to make— *Mean Streets, Taxi Driver, Raging Bull* . . . films like *The Last Temptation of Christ* and *Goodfellas*." He concludes philosophically, "I mean, who can complain?"

A recipient of the American Film Institute Life Achievement award, he was a Kennedy Center honoree in 2007 for his cultural influence. And when not making his own films, Martin Scorsese devotes much of his time to restoring classic works of cinema and preserving them for future generations of audiences.

By Alan Silverman Los Angeles 15 January 2008
Voice of America

Words and Idioms

Vocabulary
Match each word to its definition.

1. gritty *(adj)* ● l	● a. setting; environment
2. critical *(adj)* ● n	● b. intense love
3. inspired *(adj)* ● g	● c. devoted
4. surpass *(v)* ● e	● d. injurious action or force
5. asthma *(n)* ● o	● e. to exceed
6. milieu *(n)* ● a	● f. vocation
7. wry *(adj)* ● m	● g. highly motivated
8. devout *(adj)* ● c	● h. relating to judgment
9. seminary *(n)* ● n	● i. genuineness
10. calling *(n)* ● f	● j. to put into original condition
11. passion *(n)* ● b	● k. ridiculously unreasonable
12. authenticity *(n)* ● i	● l. strong; courageous
13. violence *(n)* ● d	● m. ironically humorous
14. absurd *(adj)* ● k	● n. religious school
15. restore *(n)* ● j	● o. a lung disorder

Idioms and Expressions
Fill in the blanks with the correct idiom or expression.

define (something): to set the standard; create a model
Ernest Hemingway defined American literature in the early twentieth century.

street: relating to life on public streets
Though he didn't finish school, Casey was street smart.

no doubt about: unquestionably true
She could sing well; there was no doubt about it.

1. The Beatles ___defined___ pop music for three generations.

2. "It's going to be a difficult hike," he said. "___no doubt abot___ it."

3. Henry was a tough ___Street___ fighter.

Exploring Content

A. Complete the sentence based on the reading.

1. Many think that Martin Scorsese's *Raging Bull* is the _best movie about boxing ever_

2. Scorsese's severe childhood asthma _kept him from sports_. or other activities

3. After studying in a seminary, Scorsese discovered that film _turned out to be his_. calling (true)

4. Scorsese said he was glad that he did not win an Oscar for best director early in his career because it might have _changed the kind of movies he made_

B. Choose the best answer.

1. What is the main idea of the article?
   a. Martin Scorsese didn't win an Oscar for best director until 2007, more than three decades after he started his film career.
   b. Many people, including some of his friends, think that Martin Scorsese's movies are too violent.
   c. After studying to become a priest, Martin Scorsese realized that filmmaking was his true calling.
   d. Martin Scorsese became famous for making movies that authentically portray life on the American streets.

2. What can be inferred about Martin Scorsese?
   a. Most of his movies stem from his imagination.
   b. He knows people who have been involved in organized crime.
   c. His parents were very wealthy.
   d. He did not like growing up in New York.

3. Read the following sentence.

   "Leonardo DiCaprio, who worked for the director on *The Aviator and The Departed*, says 'What I love about Mr. Scorsese's work is he not only gives the same appreciation to the entire film and the construct of the film, but he really lets the audience engage with every character, no matter how small they are'."

   Which of the following sentences best expresses the essential information in the above sentence?
   a. Leonardo DiCaprio liked working for Scorsese because of the director's attention to detail, especially concerning his films' characters.
   b. According to Leonardo DiCaprio, Scorsese gives more appreciation to constructing the film than to its characters.
   c. Leonardo DiCaprio says that Scorsese lets the audience talk with his film's characters after the movie has ended.
   d. The thing that Leonardo DiCaprio loves most about Scorsese's work is the director's appreciation of minor characters.

Summary & Discussion

Summary
Fill in the blanks.

street	authenticity	devout	define	calling
seminary	absurd	gritty	critical	asthma

Martin Scorsese's 1 _____, authentic portrayals of American 2 _____ life have made him one of the country's most revered movie directors. Scorsese acquired much of the material for his films from his childhood in New York City, during which severe 3 _____ limited his activities and gave him time to watch movies. A 4 _____Catholic, Scorsese initially went into a 5 _____ before leaving it to pursue his true 6 _____ at New York University. The 7 _____ of Scorsese's films helped 8 _____ the past four decades of American cinema. Yet despite widespread 9 _____ acclaim, Scorsese did not earn an Oscar for best director until 2007, a situation many people describe as 10 _____.

Discussion
Discuss these questions with your class.

1. Do you like the type of realistic movies that Scorsese is famous for? Why or why not?

2. Describe a famous director in your country. What type of movies does he or she make? Why do people like them? Do you like them?

3. Why do you think Scorsese did not win an Oscar for best director until 2007?

4. What impact do movies have on real life? How important are they to you and your friends?

Korean Pop Culture

Warm-up

How does something — clothes, music, a new dance, a TV show — become popular? Why do some things become very popular while others do not? In Asia, a TV drama from South Korea has sparked a "Korean wave" — a craze for Korean stars and products. This wave is so strong that women in China are even having Korean-style plastic surgery. The sudden popularity has bolstered South Korea's economy, as well as its self-esteem.

Points to Notice

As you read, look for answers as to why South Korea has become so popular. Pay attention to the comments of the following people:

• Lisa Leung — an assistant professor of cultural studies at Hong Kong's Lingnan University
• Shim Doo-bo — a South Korean instructor at National University in Singapore

Cultural Notes and Background

Korea, comprised of a peninsula surrounded by China and Japan, has been subject to invasions throughout its history. Korea was a Japanese colony from 1910 to 1945. During this period, Koreans were not allowed to speak their own language or to learn about their history. Almost as soon as Korea was liberated from Japan, the country split into two halves: North Korea and South Korea. In 1950, the north invaded the south. The United Nations sent help, and in 1953, the fighting stopped, but the country remained divided. Today, North Korea has a communist government, and South Korea has formed a republic. South Korea's economy developed rapidly between the mid-1980s and 2000. Today, it has the 12th-largest economy in the world.

Reading

Asia Goes Crazy Over Korean Pop Culture

South Korean actress Lee Young-ae attends a news conference in Hong Kong on May 21, 2005. Lee's recent television drama, "Dae Jang Geum" (*Jewel In The Palace*), achieved the highest television viewership rating in Hong Kong and South Korea.

(Korea. REUTERS/Kin Cheung)

The hottest thing in Asian pop culture these days is South Korea. The so-called Korean wave covers the craze for South Korean TV dramas, movies, and pop singers — but increasingly also for fashion, cosmetics, and electronics. 5

The Korean drama *Jewel in the Palace* clocked up record television ratings in China, Hong Kong, and Taiwan last year. Even Chinese President Hu Jintao admitted to being a fan of the historical drama about a cook at Korea's royal court. The 10 show's actors have become mega stars across Asia.

South Korea has been exporting movies and TV dramas since the late 1990s. Many Asian TV networks initially bought them because the glossy productions were comparatively cheap. 15 But audiences from China to the Philippines soon got hooked.

Lisa Leung is assistant professor of cultural studies at Hong Kong's Lingnan University. She says one of the reasons for the dramas' strong 20 appeal is that, unlike Western productions, they are culturally close to Asian viewers.

"Audiences can not only identify with the skin color, the hair color, the similar faces and looks of Korean actors and actresses but also the kind 25 of values expressed in these TV dramas," she explained. "More to the point, the kind of stress on familial values, the filial piety, the love between siblings, and friendship and all these elements that might make Korean television dramas so 30 popular in Asia."

South Korean pop stars, like the singer BoA, have also achieved cult status in many Asian countries. One young woman in Hong Kong looks for magazines and posters featuring her favorite 35 pop star, the South Korean singer and actor Rain.

"I like him, I'm his big fan," she said. "He dances great and he sings great. And his performance in the drama is good as well."

The popularity of South Korean films and 40 music has led to a veritable craze for everything Korean across Asia.

Hong Kong street markets sell traditional Korean robes to children and some brides in China are wearing them for wedding photos. 45

Learning Korean has become increasingly popular in many Asian countries, as have Korean

South Korean superstar singer Rain waves to his fans during the opening of a Korean cosmetics store in Taipei, Taiwan. Rain has been voted the best Asian singer by the Taiwanese media and his records top the charts in Taiwan.

(AP Photo/Chiang Ying-ying)

"They reported to me that after the immense popularity of Korean television dramas and films they feel that they are better treated by local Singaporean people," said Shim Doo-bo.

In many parts of Asia, Korea has become a byword for cool. South Koreans have coined a new word to describe the phenomenon: Hallyu, meaning "Korean wave."

Mr. Shim says his country has not been slow to cash in on the craze.

"Many regional governments within Korea have built up theme parks based on the characters of Korean dramas and films and the image of [South] Korea of a country which used to be known to other countries for labor strikes or student demonstration strikes for democracy is slowly moving to cool or fashionable or dynamic," he said. "So that recently officially the [South] Korean government inaugurated a campaign of so-called dynamic Korea as its catchphrase for the tourist industry."

As Asian tourists are now visiting South Korea specifically to see the locations where popular dramas are shot, the government has organized events with famous entertainers and launched a multilingual web site with information on movies and TV dramas, actors, and filming locations.

The Korean wave is a point of national pride for South Korea. After having been colonized or overshadowed by its neighbors, Japan and China, for centuries, the country finally has the chance to outdo them on the cultural stage.

But Hallyu has also boosted South Korea's economy. In 2004, the export of film and television programs along with tourism and merchandising generated revenues totaling nearly $2 billion.

food, fashion, and cosmetics. Ms. Leung says in China the craze has even meant more people undergoing plastic surgery, as she noticed during a research trip last year.

"I found that there were more and more younger girls and also older women wanting to go through plastic surgery," she said. "They would be visiting these hospitals which stress this kind of Korean-style cosmetic technology. This is not too much of a question of wanting to look more Korean, but I think in mainland China the audience might have been affected by Korean TV dramas and that they want to look more beautiful."

Ms. Leung says advertisements featuring South Korean idols have resulted in increased sales for the country's products, such as Samsung mobile phones or LG electrical appliances.

Shim Doo-bo, a South Korean, is assistant professor of communications and new media at Singapore's National University. He says Koreans living overseas have profited from the popularity of their country's cultural exports — like the South Korean housewives he interviewed in Singapore.

By Claudia Blume Hong Kong 06 January 2006

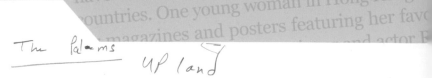

Words and Idioms

take The Palams up land

Vocabulary
Match each word to its definition.

1. hot *(adj)* ● k
2. wave *(n)* ● e
3. craze *(n)* ● p
4. cosmetic *(n)* ● i
5. mega *(adj)* ● d
6. filial *(adj)* ● n
7. piety *(n)* ● b
8. veritable *(adj)* ● l
9. robe *(n)* ● d
10. idol *(n)* ● g
11. hooked *(adj)* ● h
12. byword *(n)* ● j
13. coin *(v)* ● c
14. democracy *(n)* ● q
15. inaugurate *(v)* ● f
16. dynamic *(adj)* ● m
17. overshadow *(v)* ● o

● a. marked by greatness especially in size or degree
● b. the condition of acting correctly, or righteously
● c. to invent or create a new word or expression
● d. a long, flowing item of clothing
● e. a surge of movement or emotion
● f. to bring about the beginning of; to start
● g. a person who is highly admired and often imitated
● h. feeling the need to have or do; addicted
● i. a substance applied to a person's skin for decoration
● j. an often-used word or phrase that represents a certain idea or quality
● k. suddenly very popular
● l. true; realistic
● m. bursting with energy or new ideas; fast moving
● n. related to the relationship between children and parents
● o. to exceed in importance; to outweigh
● p. an exaggerated and often short-lived enthusiasm
● q. a system of government in which citizens elect its members by voting

Idioms and Expressions
Fill in the blanks with the correct idiom or expression.

clock up: to officially record or register; to accumulate
He is clocking up a lot of frequent-flyer miles because he travels a lot for business.

cult status: the condition of being adored or worshipped by many people
Her series of novels about a school for wizards has elevated her to cult status among young readers everywhere.

to cash in on something: to reap financial reward
Many of the small shops and restaurants near the conference center are hoping to cash in on the upcoming events there.

1. The Beatles were one of the first rock bands to achieve _cult status_ worldwide.

2. The electronics company _to cash_ on the cell-phone craze.

3. That company has _clock up_ $1 million in penalties and fines so far.

Exploring Content

A. Two of the following statements are FALSE according to the passage. Check (✔) the FALSE statements:

1. __ South Korea has been exporting movies and TV dramas since the late 1980s.
2. __ One reason Korean TV dramas are so popular is that they have cultural appeal to Asian viewers.
3. __ The Korean craze has led to an increase in plastic surgery in China.
4. __ Shim Doo-bo says Korea has been slow to cash in on the craze.

Rewrite the FALSE statements using information from the passage to make them TRUE.

a) South Korea bee exporting movies and T.V dramas since the late 1990s

b) Shim Doo-bo says korea has not been slow to cash into one the craze.

B. Find a synonym in the reading.

1. Find a word in paragraph 3 that means **sleek**.

   glossy

2. Find a word in paragraph 5 that means **emphasis**.

   stress

3. Find a verb in paragraph 6 that means **attained**.

   achived

4. Find a verb in paragraph 13 that means **benefited**.

   Profite

5. Find a verb in paragraph 18 that means **began**.

   launched

Summary & Discussion

Summary
Fill in the blanks.

byword	hot	overshadowed	clocked up	idols
coined	craze	inaugurated	cosmetics	wave

Korean pop culture is 1 _hot_ in Asia right now. The explosive popularity of the Korean drama *Jewel in the Palace*, which 2 _clocked up_ record TV ratings in China, has sparked a 3 _craze_ across Asia for all things Korean. These include not only TV shows, pop singers, and movies, but also fashion, 4 _cosmetics_, and electronics. In almost all aspects of life, Korean has become a 5 _byword_ for cool. Advertisements featuring South Korean 6 _idols_ have resulted in increased sales for those products. South Koreans have even 7 _coined_ a new word to describe the phenomenon: Hallyu, which means "Korean 8 _wave_." Hallyu has not only boosted South Korea's economy, but also its self-esteem. For centuries, the country has been 9 _overshadowed_ by neighboring Japan and China. Now, however, it has 10 _inaugurated_ a tourist campaign called "Dynamic Korea" to cash in on its newfound popularity.

Discussion
Discuss these questions with your class.

1. What country's culture or imports are hot in your country at the moment? What hot cultural crazes do you remember from the past?

2. What TV shows from other countries are popular in your country? Why do you think they are popular?

3. What are some examples you have seen of how popular TV shows, films, and records have affected the economy?

4. Which actors or singers give other countries a good impression of your country's culture? Which actors or singers give a bad impression? Why?

Video Games

Warm-up

Do you like to play video games? If so, you're not alone. The popularity of online games has increased dramatically since the first video game was introduced in the 1950s. Video game systems such as PlayStation, GameCube, and XBox compete for their share of what has become a multibillion-dollar industry worldwide. Have you ever wondered how video games began, and how they are made? What effects have these games had on world culture?

Points to Notice

In this passage, practice separating fact from opinion. Carefully read the comments of video game expert Aaron Ruby and his wife, Heather Chaplin. Which comments are facts? Which are opinions? How can you tell the difference?

Cultural Notes and Background

The popularity of video games corresponds with access to personal computers. The games have surged in America as computers have become a staple component of more and more households. In China, they are played at Internet bars. Another phenomenon witnessed almost everywhere is these games being played on hand-held monitors rather than large computers. A future trend in video games is the continued development of Massively Multiplayer Online Game (MMO). This is a computer game capable of supporting hundreds, or even thousands, of players simultaneously. MMOs enable players to compete against each other on a grand scale and to sometimes interact meaningfully with people around the world.

Video Games Have Come a Long Way

Video games top many 'wish lists' this holiday season . . . and the rest of the year, too, with annual sales approaching $10 billion in the United States alone. Video and Internet games are constantly evolving, and as they do, they are changing the way people around the world play and interact.

In a relatively short period of time, video games have come a long way. That's what journalist Heather Chaplin realized when she started researching the industry's history. "We actually started all the way back in the 1950s, with a nuclear physicist who came up with the first video game for an Open House day (public relations event)," she says. From there, her research took her to "the original founders of the computer culture, people at the Massachusetts Institute of Technology in the early 1960s . . . [and to] Nolan Bushnell, who founded Atari, who was really the first person to think, 'This could be something that could be commercially viable.'"

Nolan Bushnell was right, and during the 1980s, the industry expanded. Video game expert Aaron Ruby says it reached a turning point in the mid-1990s. "I think the 'PlayStation' coming out from Sony in 1995 was what brought us to what we now think of as modern video gaming," he says. "Because once you have the PlayStation and you get into the PlayStation 2, Nintendo comes out with the GameCube. And then we have Microsoft entering the industry in 2001 with the XBox. That pretty much leads us right into the current modern situation."

Members of the news media photograph the new controller for Sony PlayStation 3 during the Sony Computer Entertainment, Inc. 2006 E3 media event at Sony Studios in Culver City, Calif., May 8, 2006. The new controller looks similar to the one for the older PlayStation 2 but adds motion sensors to detect six degrees of movement.

(AP Photo/Kevork Djansezian)

Husband and wife team Aaron Ruby and Heather Chaplin have spent the last five years visiting video game labs and designing studios, and attending almost every industry conference and gaming competition. They wanted to meet the real people who create this virtual world. "They are some of the smartest people of their generation," Mr. Ruby says. "They are people who like to use technology to bring new things to life."

"They have devoted themselves to making videogames," Ms. Chaplin says. "We spent a lot of time profiling the developing of a game called 'Star Wars Galaxies' here in the U.S. One of the programmers was at Hubble Space Telescope before coming there. I mean, we have people that have multiple degrees in physics, in psychology, in architecture."

Creating a video game, Ms. Chaplin explains, requires the talents of dozens of people. "A lot of people don't realize what a collaborative process it is," she says. "Every game designer starts at a different place in terms of how to create something fun, whether that is a character or a movement or an environment. Then, at this point, you might have up to 60- or 100- or 400-person teams: animators, coders, music people, and managers."

Mr. Ruby adds, "The programmers are representing a smaller percentage because the amount of art and other assets that are required to make a video game these days are so enormous that the artists are actually outnumbering the programmers. There is also a whole number of people whose job is simply to test each version of the game and make sure that there is no problem."

Mr. Ruby says the studios where these creative people work look and feel very different from any other workplace. "One of the cardinal rules of the game-designing studios is, you walk in and it's incredibly dim," he says. "They like to work in dim conditions where they can see their monitors. And it's always very cool in there to keep the computers functioning at their peak."

What is usually a relaxing atmosphere, Ms. Chaplin says, can turn into a stressful one when the team is racing to meet a deadline. "It's a known thing that deadlines are almost impossible to meet," she says. "So, if you come anywhere within say, six months of a game deadline, they might be working 80 hours a week, living off pizza, diet Coke. It's really an interesting environment."

Video games are a global business. Japan has been contributing to the industry for more than three decades, but Aaron Ruby notes that other Asian countries are now entering the market. "China and Korea, and Koreans in particular, are really starting to develop their own games industry to the extent that they are now starting to move beyond their own market into the western markets," he says. "I think the Korean games, as they move west, have the potential to offer a lot to the game designing community in terms of innovation."

Like other types of entertainment, Mr. Ruby says, video games are changing American culture. "For example, in America, for a long time, play has not been culturally accepted, the way it is maybe in Japan, where the notion of families sitting down and playing together is kind of much more culturally approved," he says. "For example, when Nintendo Entertainment System came out in America, they had to call it the NES, Nintendo Entertainment System, rather than Famicom, which is what they call it in Japan, because they realized that Americans would be turned off by the notion of families playing together. I think that kind of thing is changing. The notion of play as an important part of life and a potential social activity is really increasing."

Not only can video games bring families together, he says, they can bring people from different cultures closer to each other. "I can go online and play with a friend who lives in Istanbul, who is maybe a teenager," he says. "And we maybe end up hooking up with somebody from Asia who is rather old. We can all get together and share things and experiences that bring us all together."

The more innovative and creative ideas there are, the more new and exciting games are released . . . and the more competitive this global market gets every year.

A figurine of the character Jack, from the movie 'Nightmare Before Christmas' is displayed at an event held by software company Square Enix Co. Ltd. The exhibit unveiled new game content for Sony's PlayStation 3 and Nintendo's Wii next generation gaming consoles during the 2006 E3 Video Game Convention in Hollywood, California May 8, 2006.

(REUTERS/Lucas Jackson)

By Faiza Elmasry 20 December 2005

Vocabulary

Match each word to its definition.

1. top *(v)* ●	● a. to allocate or commit resources to a cause or activity
2. evolve *(v)* ●	● b. to produce a detailed outline of something
3. relatively *(adv)* ●	● c. able to produce new and imaginative ideas or work
4. founder *(n)* ●	● d. to have first priority or occupy the primary position
5. viable *(adj)* ●	● e. a person who starts or establishes something
6. devote *(v)* ●	● f. more than one; many
7. profile *(v)* ●	● g. able to be successful; possible
8. multiple *(adj)* ●	● h. a new idea, method, or device
9. collaborative *(adj)* ●	● i. worked on by more than one person or group
10. animator *(n)* ●	● j. a resource; a beneficial item or quality
11. asset *(n)* ●	● k. in comparison to expectations
12. version *(n)* ●	● l. the highest level or greatest degree
13. creative *(adj)* ●	● m. a concept; an idea
14. dim *(adj)* ●	● n. to change naturally over time
15. peak *(n)* ●	● o. in low light; not bright
16. innovation *(n)* ●	● p. an artist who creates animated drawings
17. notion *(n)* ●	● q. a slightly different copy of something

Idioms and Expressions

Fill in the blanks with the correct idiom or expression.

wish list: a list of things a person would ideally like to have
An experienced goal keeper is one of the items on the team's wish list this year.

turning point: the specific time when an important and usually positive change begins
Their rocky relationship reached a turning point when they started attending marriage counseling sessions.

cardinal rule: a basic principle or fundamental law
It's a cardinal rule not to talk in class while the teacher is lecturing.

1. The president's _____ includes world peace and cleaner air.

2. The _____ of baseball is to never look away from the ball.

3. Winning the essay competition was a _____ in his scholastic career.

Exploring Content

A. Two of the following statements are FALSE according to the passage. Check (✔) the FALSE statements:

1. __ According to video game expert Aaron Ruby, Nintendo's GameCube in 1995 began the modern age of video games.

2. __ Japan has been making video games for more than 30 years.

3. __ In the making of a new video game, programmers always outnumber artists.

4. __ Japanese families traditionally play games together more often than American families.

Rewrite the FALSE statements using information from the passage to make them TRUE.

a) _____

b) _____

B. Choose the best answer.

1. What is the main idea of the article?
   a. It takes many people to create modern video games.
   b. Video games are a worldwide phenomenon.
   c. The evolution of video games is changing American culture.
   d. Modern video games are very different from the original ones.

2. What can be inferred about the Chinese video game industry?
   a. It is the second strongest in Asia.
   b. It is the fastest-growing video game industry in the world.
   c. It will never be as strong as America's.
   d. It lags behind Korea and Japan.

3. Read the following sentence:

   "Video game expert Aaron Ruby says [the industry] reached a turning point in the mid-1990s."

   Which of the following sentences best expresses the essential information in the above sentence?
   a. The video game industry began to boom in the mid-1990s.
   b. The video game industry began to slump in the mid-1990s.
   c. Until the mid-1990s, video games were very popular.
   d. Until the mid-1990s, American families did not play video games.

Summary
Fill in the blanks.

viable	evolved	turning point	relatively	founder
wish lists	top	collaborative	innovation	notion

Video games have **1** _____ from novelty experiments to a commercially

2 _____ industry since their introduction in the 1950s. In this **3** _____ short

period, making video games has changed from a one-person design team to a **4** _____

process involving hundreds of people. As **5** _____ increases, artists are out-

numbering programmers on game-design teams. Nolan Bushnell, the **6** _____ of

Atari, was the first person to see the commercial potential of video games. The industry

expanded in the 1980s, then hit a **7** _____ in the mid-1990s with the introduction

of the Sony PlayStation; this was soon followed by GameCube and XBox, which led towards

the current situation. Today, video games **8** _____ children's **9** _____, and

there are many adults and college students who also like to play. Aaron Ruby, a video-game

expert, says that American families, who may once have been turned off by the

10 _____, may soon end up playing video games together as a family activity.

Discussion
Discuss these questions with your class.

1. How often do you play video games? Which ones are your favorites?

2. In your opinion, what are the features of a good video game?

3. How can video games bring families and people from different cultures closer together? Explain.

4. Why do you think video games are so popular worldwide?